PRAYERS THAT ANNIHILATE THE ENEMY
| VOLUME 1

PRAYERS THAT ANNIHILATE THE ENEMY | VOLUME 1

PRAYERS FOR THE BODY, MIND, SPIRIT, AND SOUL

LACHAUN STRONG

CONTENTS

Forward: By Tony Anthony Strong

"When you're destined for..." These words acknowledge some of the beautiful things that the author of this book has done. She also happens to be my lovely wife, Apostle Lachaun Strong. Since the day I met her, she has always been driven to bring much-needed change to this world.

We met over a phone call. I was looking for construction shoring equipment that I needed to complete a project. I had no idea I was speaking to the love of my life. There was something special about her. From the first time I called her office, she treated me like a repeat customer by doing whatever she could to help me meet my deadline. She stayed in contact with me until the problem was resolved. I could hear something special in her voice, so I asked if we could meet. And, of course, at first, she said no, but eventually, she agreed.

Making that phone call was one of the best decisions of my life. God brought me a rare jewel—an intercessor and a servant of God—for which I am extremely grateful. I've never met someone like her who loves Jesus like she does. From the first time I met her in person, we formed an immediate bond, and the rest is our history. I knew she was "the one" to take to meet Mama. I wanted a wife. I wanted a prayer warrior and someone who loved me unconditionally.

Knowing my wife has caused me to mature, grow, and heal in areas in which I didn't know I needed healing. She is an encourager, a motivator, and a fighter. I love that she refuses to give up and allows the enemy to defeat her. My wife's spirit is her destiny all by itself. She is God's gift to the body of Christ as a strong intercessor and prayer warrior. I hear her pray and cry to God for the people morning, noon, and night. She has such a passionate desire to see and show others that they can experience the Lord Jesus just as she has. If I had to put into words a phrase that describes her, I would say, "Success breeds success." She is successful because she allows God to consistently do work on her day by day.

She is very self-reflective and always desires for God to get the glory in her life. Pride doesn't live within her at all. I always hear her say this: "I'm at the Father's feet."

My life changed because of her full yes to God. I want to thank my wife for being who she is. I am proud of what God is doing through your life. You will forever have my support and prayers. I vow to continue to cover you in prayer and support you in all you do in righteousness as you and I walk this new journey. I love you, babe. I am proud to have you on my arm and that you have my last name. Keep climbing. God is blessing you, our marriage, and our ministry to reach new levels.

May the following words from the author inspire change and elevate you to new heights. After reading this book of prayers, you will learn not just how to fight but also how to war.

Blessings
Prophet Tony Anthony Strong

To God

I must first give thanks to God, the Father of all Creation in Heaven. Abba, you are amazing, and I love You more than life. Thank You for not giving up on me. I never thought that I would be able to write a book, but from my creation in Heaven and my descent down to earth, You have always shown Yourself strong in me and loved me no matter what. Thank You, God, for allowing me to really have a real God encounter with You. Your pure, undefiled love for me has pushed me to dig deeper and thirst for You like never before. I'm forever changed by Your presence, and I will forever remain at Your feet.

To My Husband

To my wonderful husband. I thank God for you every day. Thank you so much for wiping my tears, praying for me through restless nights, telling me to keep fighting, and showing me that I could do all things through Christ who strengthens me. Thank you for not abandoning me during one of the most difficult times of my life, even though you didn't understand everything I was birthing at that moment. You covered me spiritually and naturally. You are my best friend, prayer partner, lover, and the greatest husband a woman could have. I honor you and will continue to submit to you as your wife. I love you, my earthly king.

To My Spiritual Parents and Overseers

I want to thank Dr. Edison and Mattie Nottage. I am so glad that I met you. Because of my obedience to God and my coming to the Bahamas, God changed my life forever. I knew that I was dying, and I needed to get help from a general in the spirit. You and your staff didn't judge me and loved me to life. I thank God for the deliverance that I received at your ministry. The witchcraft that was put on me by all five of the agents of Satan was sent to kill me, but God used you to help me get free and to cast the devil out. Thank you for sharing yourself with the world while treating everyone with a sense of belonging. I am submitted to your teaching, love, and correction.

You and Apostle Eddison are jewels in the earth and such a blessing to the kingdom of God. Thank you for living what you preach! I love you so much and honor you both, Dr. Mattie Nottage and Dr. Apostle Edison Nottage. You ARE my spiritual parents, and you will never have a problem with me submitting to the truth of God's Word flowing out of you and your leadership. Thank you.

PREFACE

<u>How it ALL began</u>

I must start this book by stating that it was born through one of my life's biggest upward spiritual Apostolic thrusts. The faith that I thought I had was tried and proven. God had to show me that Hell truly is real, and that Satan has come to kill, steal, and destroy. God has shown me that Hell runs through a false power. That false power is the dark power of witchcraft. Yes, witchcraft is real, and many believers in Christ Jesus refuse to discuss this topic and refuse to speak about it until they realize that it's real. Often, it's not until it's their time to be free from that level of bondage that they will accept that it is real. It is amazing how much witchcraft is floating around on Earth and being released from Hell every day. The Bible states in Isaiah 5:13–14 (AMP), "Therefore My people go into exile because they lack knowledge [of God]. And their honorable men are famished, and their common people are parched with thirst. Therefore Sheol (the realm of the dead) has increased its appetite and opened its mouth beyond measure; And [a]Jerusalem's splendor, her multitude, her [boisterous] uproar, and her [drunken] revelers descend into it."

We must take the Word of God as being the true living Word. The Bible clearly states that the people of God who are refusing truth, holiness, and a life of consecration to the Father are preparing themselves for Sheol, which is Hell. Hell is enlarging itself daily to swallow up the rebellious and those who are willing to open up to the truth. We must not only accept Jesus Christ as our Lord and Savior but also accept His truth, which is His Word. The Bible also states in Hosea 4:6 (KJV), "My people are destroyed for lack of knowledge: because thou hast rejected knowledge, I will also reject thee, that thou shalt be no priest to me: seeing thou hast forgotten the law of thy God, I will also forget thy children. Rejecting the truth will destroy you and those who are connected to you. It's time for the church of the Lord Jesus Christ to take a stand, speak out, and pray against all forms of evil, including witchcraft.

Remember, Satan cannot create, only duplicate. He is a mimicker. Witchcraft is a false power, a mimic of the Holy Spirit. The Bible states in Psalms 62:11–12, "God has spoken once, Twice I have heard this: That power belongs to God. Also, to You, O Lord belongs mercy; For You render to each one according to his work." God is all-powerful and has conquered death, Hell, and the grave. No, we are not to walk around looking for witches and warlocks; that's not what I am saying, but I am aware that 80% of the people within the church and world are bound by this spirit one way or another. Church of the Lord Jesus Christ, wake up!! The realization that there are real agents of Satan—full-fledged witches, warlocks, grand high priests, etc.—changed my prayer life forever. When God broke the scales off my eyes I could now see what was really around me in the spiritual realm. This is when I entered one of the biggest wars of my life. I had to learn to fight or die. I have always been a fighter and knew I didn't want to die. Jesus

Christ's power is greater than any demon, devil, ruler of darkness, or principality. I was able to overcome and stay free through real power, which is the power of God.

During this season, God showed me demonic things that I wasn't aware I was carrying as an Apostle of the Lord Jesus Christ. God totally broke me and stripped me of all that I thought I knew. He broke the stronghold of religiosity out of my life, which propelled me to experience Him in such a beautiful and glorious way! There was a new mandate from Heaven for my life! God broke me completely down to bring total, real deliverance into my life. He delivered me from "me!" This crushing, bruising, and beating brought forth a pure, genuine oil that would eventually touch nations.

This book will help you realize that the real oil of God is produced through honesty, brokenness, and determination. I will be ministering to 4 main components that are foundational for anyone who is amid learning about spiritual warfare and for those who need to be sharpened in the area of spiritual warfare. Get ready! You are about to learn how to war!

We will look at the mind, body, spirit, and soul with subgroups. The Father loves us so much and desires that we become everything He has created us to be. He desires for us to grow from every test and trial we encounter. Tests should be fuel for every believer in Christ Jesus to ignite the holy fire, produce genuine humility, and produce pure oil in us. A touch from the Father will forever change the life of anyone that we are assigned to, with the love of Jesus Christ.

INTRODUCTION

The prayers in this book are downloads from Heaven that the Lord gave me to pray myself out of some of the most difficult things and attacks of my life. They literally saved my life. I learned quickly that peace, healing, deliverance, and love are all found in his presence. When I come to Him, I only need to surrender and obey; He will do the rest. I had to learn to live in a place where my ear was pressed to His mouth. It was either to follow the Father's directions or die! I thank God for this season of my life; it taught me how to war. I'm so grateful for Jesus Christ!

I will also be teaching you how to engage in strategic warfare prayers that will help you come out of any attack you may be under in your life. You may not be going through anything right now, but as you surrender to Jesus Christ, there will be mandated attacks that you will go through as a believer in Christ Jesus. Don't allow it to mentally destroy you, though. Don't be discouraged. The fiery trail that you may be on at this moment was only sent by the enemy to cause the growth of God in your life. The Bible tells us in Peter 4:1 (KJV): "Therefore since Christ suffered for us in the flesh, arm yourselves also with the same mind, for he who has suffered in the flesh has ceased from sin." We must make a conscious decision to live for Jesus Christ (for real) and not play with our walk with him. This kind of surrender to the Father launches attacks of all kinds upon your life. As soon as you give God a genuine yes, you are automatically enlisted in the army of the Lord. We must know that whatever we are faced with, Jesus is with us and will never leave or forsake us. We must be reminded that the blood of Jesus Christ works, and His Word is potent, full of Holy Ghost power, and able to deliver anyone in need. When you stand praying to the Father with a pure heart, God will come to your rescue. Just trust Him. We are in a real war; the spirit realm is real, and the inhabitants of the earth are merely pawns on the chessboard of Heaven. There really isn't a comparison of who will win because Jesus Christ is already the champ! He has already conquered death, Hell, and the grave! Hallelujah!!!

Now, there is a prerequisite for you as a believer in Christ Jesus to get results: you must believe that God hears and answers prayers. The Bible tells us in Mark 11:24 (KJV): "Therefore I say unto you, whatever things you desire, when you pray, believe that you will receive them, and you shall have them." If you are praying and fasting and do not believe that God will answer you every time you sacrifice to speak to God in the name of Jesus Christ, your prayers are null and void and will have no results. It is a waste of your time. Go ahead and eat. We must believe that God is able to meet us at every point of our need when we talk to Him in prayer. God is able!

1

LET'S GO!

Warriors, I will walk you through some effective ways to get results in prayer and reveal to you secrets from Heaven that the believers in Christ Jesus have ignored or have not been made privy to for a long time. We must now pray with strategy, accuracy, and precision. We can no longer pray amiss and waste time. Mediocre religious prayers will no longer work. We must pray prayers saturated with FIRE! The Bible states in James 5:16–16, "Confess your faults one to another, and pray one for another, that ye may be healed. The effectual fervent prayer of a righteous man availeth much." Cute prayers do not work! Shy prayers do not work when you are in trouble! There must be a cry unto Jesus Christ from the pit of your belly that screams, Jesus Christ, help me! He will come to your rescue when you call upon Him! Jesus Christ is soon to come, and we must declare Heaven on earth through our prayers and intercession. Titles don't matter in the presence of the Lord. We should come to Him as dear children and allow Him to totally make us whole. When we allow the Lord to gut us out, we receive His oil to cast and pray the devil out in Jesus

Christ's name. God's desire is for His children to be free while serving and bringing Him glory on earth.

I encourage every believer in Christ Jesus to remain humble and broken in the presence of God, no matter how long you have been saved. There is always more that we can obtain from the Lord. God really has humbled me during the last season of my life, and I will forever remain at His feet. I encourage you, as a purified apostolic voice on earth, to do the same. Remaining at His feet brought me out of bondage and keeps me out of bondage. I'm releasing a clarion call in the spirit even now. I call forth all of the warriors of God out of bondage and back into intercession. Midwives, intercessors, come out of the caves! You are not crazy. What you have been feeling, sensing, and experiencing in the spirit realm is real. We, the church, are in a full-fledged war. Let's put on the entire armor of God, and let's war and win!

First, let's give thanks

Father, you are love. You are merciful, and Your grace is absolutely amazing. Thank You for being the Lord of our lives. Thank You for being a gentle Father who protects, delivers, and sets the captive free! Thank You for Your salvation and the precious blood You shed for us. Thank You for not giving us what we deserve. You sacrificed Yourself for us on the cross and became a curse, so we didn't have to be cursed. You are the Rose of Sharon, the bright morning star, our healer, deliverer, and sustainer. We love you, Jesus! We thank You for taking care of us day by day. We thank You for filling us with Your Spirit and comforting us through every storm. We thank You for redeeming us from the hands of the enemy and restoring us to You.

We declare that You are the Lord. We declare that You are

King and ruler over everything. We acknowledge Your sovereignty! Lover of our souls, our purpose, and our great deliver, we humbly prepare for war and know that as we march into battle, You are with us. Cloth us with Your armor. Cover us with Your blood and mantle us with Your anointing for victory in this war. We are ready to go to war and win. In Jesus Christ's name, we pray, amen.

2

HITTING THE TARGET

In order for the believer in Christ Jesus to be effective, we must follow the instructions that God has given us in His Word. 1 Timothy 2:1-2 tells us to FIRST pray for those in authority. We will do that, but there are some key things that we must do before that. The Lord has shown me that many of the saints are not praying with strategy.

When a football team prepares to play against their opponent, they study the team so that they can play to win and not just for fun. Always remember that the object of the game is to win. I shared with you earlier that we are in a war, and Jesus will soon return to get His bride. To get effective results, we must be detailed and direct in our prayers. Bullseye. The devil doesn't play fair, hence why we cannot afford to guess or even play trivial games when it's time to go to war, but we must know, see, and hear clearly in order to defeat the enemy. General prayers are not sufficient for what has been released on earth from Hell to destroy the saints of God. Fasting and prayer can't be something you do when it's convenient for you anymore. It must be a lifestyle.

In this dispensation, in order for your prayers to not be

blocked, there must be some foundational things adhered to consistently so that your prayers are not counteracted by the enemy. Doing so will guarantee that you will get results from God, our Father in Heaven. Remember, the Bible says that Satan comes to kill, steal, and destroy. Every true believer in Christ Jesus has a hit on their life from Hell. Satan's desire is for you to fail at everything that you do. But it's God's will for you to have life and have it more abundantly in every area of your life. We see an example of this in Daniel 10:13 when Daniel had prayed for twenty-one days, but his breakthrough was held up due to the Prince of Persia blocking answers from coming down and being deposited into Daniel's spirit while he was in his time of consecration unto the Lord. When we go into prayer, we must ensure that we get rid of the demons and principalities that have been sent to block, stop, and hinder the believers in Christ Jesus from getting their breakthroughs.

The prayer below is a good one that the Lord gave me to stop the enemy from snatching my prayers before they hit Heaven's atmosphere.

3

____

PREPARING THE ATMOSPHERE BEFORE INTERCESSION | TILLING THE GROUND.

Father God, in Jesus's name, we thank You, Lord, for who You are to us and for Your amazing love. We thank You for the blood of Jesus Christ, which sets us free from any bondage and destroys Satan and all of his demons and principalities. We ask for forgiveness for our sins and that You take Your blood and wash us inside and out. Don't allow anything within us to hinder us from Your sacred presence. We repent of all sins, knowingly and unknowingly. Wash us so we may enter Your presence clean, in Jesus Christ's name.

<u>The Legal Blood of Jesus Christ| Destroying Demonic Surveillance systems.</u>

God, Your Word declares in Proverbs 15:3, "The eyes of the LORD are in every place, beholding both the good and evil." Jesus, we ask that You watch over us and cover us with Your blood. Cover every wall, window, window seal, door, and threshold with Your Blood. We release the legal blood of

Jesus Christ to be in the atmosphere of our homes, to bleed from the walls, and to even come up through the floors. In every foundational part of our homes and lives, we release the legal blood of Jesus Christ to cover them all in Jesus Christ's name.

Father, any monitoring spirit, familiar spirit, third eye, or demonic GPS systems that are utilized to watch, listen, monitor, or record our prayers for interference purposes, may they all be burned by the holy fire of Jesus Christ. We release the fire of God to burn to a crisp every third eye that is on assignment from Satan to seek us out for demise. Father, we thank You that every demonic GPS navigation system from the gates of Hell is destroyed. We ask that Your Holy Spirit confuse it, stop it from completely working, and fry every component that it runs on in Jesus Christ's name. We render it powerless and dysfunctional in the name of Jesus Christ.

We disassemble, dismantle, disable, and destroy that demonic GPS system in the name of Jesus Christ. Father, I thank You that no agents of Satan will not Astro project, translate, or appear in our surroundings, homes, jobs, and ministries in Jesus's name. May the demonic maps that they put together to search out the righteous, pure people of God be roasted by fire now in the name of Jesus Christ. May the demonic silent "pull-ups" at homes, ministries, businesses, jobs, and schools be exposed in Jesus's name. For the Lord, our God, is our refuge; in Him will we trust. We shine the light of Jesus Christ on the enemy and his pawns now, in the name of Jesus Christ. Expose yourself, reveal yourself, and stand still to receive the punishment and judgment of God. The Word declares, "Touch not mine anointed and do my prophets no harm," which makes you illegal. You will not plan silent attacks to sabotage and wreak havoc on our lives in Jesus's name. For the Word of God declares that every high thing will be brought down in Jesus' name. Fall Satan! Fall, in Jesus Christ's name, amen!

<u>Using the Hammer of God</u>

Lord, Your Word declares that You have given us the hammer of the Lord in Jeremiah 23:29. We boldly take the hammer of God and destroy every demonic wall that the Satanists put up for protection to block our prayers and petitions from getting to You in Jesus Christ's name. May every barrier and glass ceiling put in place against our prayers and intercession be broken now, in Jesus Christ's name. We will remain focused on our assignments, purpose, and the God-given mandates You entrust us with. We rebuke, refuse, and disallow distractions, wrongful thoughts, daily tasks, issues in our bodies, gossip, phone calls, social media, or even family members who may try to pull us from Your presence. This time is for You! Every barrier, be burned by fire now, in Jesus Christ's name. Every wall, we command you to fall down now in Jesus Christ's name. We will war and win! We take back our families, communities, and nation in Jesus Christ's name. Nothing will hinder us from being laser-focused on intercession and prayer.

~

<u>Forgiveness</u>

Father, we forgive all those who have hurt us, knowingly and unknowingly. Dearest Jesus, the Word of God declares in Ephesians 4:32, "Be kind and compassionate to one another, forgiving each other, just as in Christ God forgave you." Father, help us to remember that Your blood works for anyone who receives it as we pray. We understand that remembering this Lord, will help us pray with compassion and strategy. We declare and decree that our prayer lives will not be hindered or blocked because of unforgiveness. We refuse to miss You, oh God.

Thank you

Because of unforgiveness, grudges, and other things that act as barriers to You. We desire you, and we utilize our weapon of war, the hammer of God, to completely crush the barrier of unforgiveness into powder forever.

Ruah of God scatter that demonic powder of unforgiveness in the wind, never to return again. We will pray with freedom in our hearts in Jesus Christ's name, amen!

~

<u>The Fire of God</u>

Father, we thank You for being a consuming fire, according to Hebrews 12:29. We thank You that when we call upon You, You will show up and break every chain, shackle, and fetter. Father cover us with your holy blood and fire as we intercede for your people in the name of Jesus Christ. May Your fire cover our homes, families, friends, ministries, and communities. May Your fire be a barrier against retaliation and backlash from our time of intercession with You today. We release the fire of God as a sweet deliverer in Your presence today. We command every dark, evil entity sent from Hell to bring strange fire to the life of every believer to be destroyed with the fire of God, now in Jesus Christ's name. You are illegal! We declare and decree that everything and everyone attached to us is covered with the fire of God.

We thank You for Your prayers of fire, oh God! We thank You for effectual prayers, according to James 5:16 (KJV). We thank You that when we pray with Your fire, we will get instant results in Jesus Christ's name. We release the fire of God to blind the wicked, including enemies, all forms of darkness, witches, warlocks, shapeshifters, Nephilim spirits, and dead disembodied spirits in Jesus Christ's name. For the Word of God declares that God is a consuming fire. You will not shapeshift into any form of animal, bird, or reptile to spy, attack, or watch us in Jesus's name. You will not counteract any prayer that we release before the Father in Jesus's name.

I command you, in the name of Jesus Christ, to choke on your own venom, Satan, along with all of your demon spirits. I command the glory of God to blind you. You will be tortured by your own trouble and destroyed mightily with the heavy Word of God. May your feet be burned with the fire of God, and may your throat be slit with the sword of the spirit. May your head be crushed to pieces with the shield of faith. May your loins be ripped in half to prevent you from reproducing your own kind. May your feet be broken, and you will remain crippled, hopeless, and helpless in Jesus's name.

~

Releasing the Angels of the Lord, The Defenders of the Faith

Lord, thank You for Your holy angels. I release them to come now and surround us as we pray and declare God's holy Word over our atmospheres and ministries. Angels of the Lord, defenders of the Faith, come now with your swords, shields, and wings dipped in the legal blood of Jesus drawn back, ready to do battle on our behalf. We release you to fight and annihilate anything that is not like God in Jesus Christ's name. Stand on every wall shoulder to shoulder, foot to foot, ankle to ankle, with your heavy artillery in your hands. We release you to war on our behalf, in Jesus Christ's name. Angels of the Lord, we release you to bring valves of oil to bring healing and deliverance. Angels of the Lord destroy anything that doesn't bring the Father's glory into our midst. God, we trust you! In Jesus Christ's name!

∾

<u>Releasing the Lion of Judah</u>

Dearest Jesus, come as the Lion of Judah and watch over us as we pray to You, Lord. Smite down any demon that tries to block us from hearing Your voice, that tries to make us sleepy, fatigued, and tired during intercession with Your mighty paw in Jesus Christ's name. I declare and decree freedom in our minds, hearts, and spirits in the name of Jesus Christ. Father, I thank You that I am filled with Your Holy Spirit, and I will pray for what You have declared over my life in Your Word in Jesus Christ's name.

Father, I thank You that, as I intercede and pray for Your people, mighty miracles, signs, and wonders will follow. Father, I thank You that Your blood will heal every broken body, every broken mind, every broken spirit, and save every broken soul. Father, I thank You that You hear us in Jesus Christ's name, amen.

4

———

PRAYING FOR THOSE IN LEADERSHIP

As the world continues to evolve into something very demonic in the last days before the return of Christ, it's the job of every baptized believer in Christ Jesus to stand boldly and continue to pray for those that God is allowing to be in leadership on earth. We are to pray for them and not destroy them with our words. We are to love them and not hate them for the decisions they make on earth. This is why it is very important for every believer across the United States and the world to stand together as one in prayer and intercession. The Bible tells us in Psalms 133:1 (KJV), "Behold, how good and how pleasant it is for brethren to dwell together in unity." When we stand together in unity, we can defeat the enemy and cover our leadership in this earthen realm, as the Lord told us to do.

In 1 Timothy 2:1–4, the Bible states this: "First of all, then, I urge that supplications, prayers, intercessions, and thanksgivings be made for all people, for kings and all who are in high positions, that we may lead a peaceful and quiet life, godly and dignified in every way." This is good, and it is pleasing in the sight of God our Savior, who desires all people to be saved and to come to the knowledge of the truth. The Word of God clearly instructs the intercessor and even those who are not intercessors to make supplications, prayers, intercessions, and thanksgiving to the Lord for those whom He has called into leadership. We are not to pray for what we want, but we are to pray as the Word instructs us to. Our prayers should never be based on color, creed, culture, opinions, hearsay, news media, or even our own desires and beliefs. Being a leader is not an easy job, so we must pray with compassion and with the love of Jesus Christ in our hearts. Let's begin this prayer by praying for leadership on earth in Jesus Christ's name first.

Father, we thank You for everyone that You have allowed to be in leadership in this earthly realm. Father, Your Word declares in James 5:16 to "Confess your faults one to another, and pray one for another, that ye may be healed. The effectual fervent prayer of a righteous man availeth much." We cover them earnestly and fervently with righteous prayers.

Father, we thank You as a nation and as the body of Christ for giving us the privilege to come together and intercede on behalf of our leadership. We thank You for allowing them to serve our country and be appointed for such a time as this. Thank You, oh God, that they are covered with the legal blood of Jesus Christ. I thank You, God, that we, as believers, will see everyone through the eyes of you, Father in the name of Jesus Christ.

Father, we thank You for every king, queen, mayor, governor, treasurer, and secretary of state in the name of Jesus Christ. We thank You for the Congress. We thank You for the president of our country. We thank You, Lord, for police officers. We thank You, Lord, for the firemen. We thank You, Lord, for those in leadership positions in the medical field. We thank You for nursing home administrators, chief nursing officers, directors, and VPs of medical facilities in the name of Jesus Christ. We thank You, Lord, for the judges. We thank You, Lord, for governors. We thank You, Lord, for principals in schools. We thank You for deans of colleges. We thank You, Father, for supervisors, directors, and vice presidents of corporations in Jesus Christ's name. Father, we ask that You guide them to lead in accordance with Your Word. We thank You, Lord, that they will not rule with an iron fist, but they will have compassion on people across this world in the name of Jesus Christ. I thank You, Lord, that everyone you have allowed to be in leadership will lead with love, compassion, grace, mercy, and peace in Jesus Christ's name. I thank You, Lord, that everyone that You call into leadership will not be biased, will not be racist, and will not be prejudiced. We declare and decree that they will make good decisions no matter what culture or creed the person comes from.

Father, we pray that You cover judges in courthouse systems who are allowed to make decisions that can affect the lives of many daily. I pray, Father, that Your love will find them and that Your grace will lead them to do the right, moral, and just thing towards those who are on trial. I thank You, Father, that judges or lawyers will pad cases and give wrongful sentencing based on lies and bribes in Jesus Christ's name. Thank You, Father, that judges will not work the system for their own good or the good of those they know. I thank You, Father, that judges will make integral decisions concerning sentencing someone to prison or even jail time in the name of Jesus Christ. Thank You, Lord, that they have sharp discernment. I thank You that they will be able to lead with Your heart in the name of Jesus Christ. Father, we thank You that police officers are only led by Your Spirit. I pray, oh God, that You will protect our police officers from all hurt, harm, and danger in the name of Jesus Christ. I pray that they will remain focused on their shifts, remain integral in our communities, and be one of the many pillars that humanity can depend upon.

Father, I pray that You will pour out a special blessing upon police officers for their willingness to serve their country and their cities and put their lives on the line for regular people every day in Jesus Christ's name. I pray that they're protected and covered by the legal blood of Jesus Christ every day. I thank You that they will go home to their families healthy, whole, and alive after every shift, in the name of Jesus Christ. I thank You that police officers are not corrupt in the name of Jesus Christ. We demolish by the legal blood of Jesus Christ, the demon of Astaroth. I thank You, Father, that police officers will lead with peace, not chaos. I thank You that police officers will not cause confusion but will demonstrate Your love for all people. Your Word declares in 1 Corinthians 16:14, "…and whatever you do, do it with kindness and love." I thank You that the hearts of police officers are saturated with Your love. I thank You that they will love the community, cultures, people, and themselves. I thank You that the gates of their minds are not traumatized, terrorized, delusional, or full of fear. I thank You that they live in peace and love for all mankind, in Jesus Christ's name. I thank You, God, that they are spirit-filled and that there's no place for anything demonic in their lives. I thank You, Father, that police officers are strong pillars of the community in the name of Jesus Christ. I thank You, Father, for breaking the rage of every police officer across the globe in the name of Jesus Christ. I thank You that police officers will not be paranoid or trigger-happy but will love, protect, and serve their local communities in the name of Jesus Christ. We drive all fear away from the gates of their minds and hearts in the name of Jesus Christ. Father, walk with them daily and take them back home safely in the name of Jesus Christ.

Father, thank You for the leaders of countries. May all presidents, queens, kings, governors, mayors, and congressmen lead with integrity and lead well. May they serve the people of this earth with purity of heart, wisdom, and understanding. May they make good decisions, righteous decisions, and just decisions for the people. Father, I thank You that Your Word declares in Proverbs 21:9 that, "The king's heart is in the hand of the Lord, as the rivers of water: he turneth it whithersoever he will."

Father, I thank You that every president, king, queen, governor, mayor, and congressman hears your voice concerning the people of the earth. I thank You that You will turn their hearts away from corruption, disaster, and destruction. I thank You that they will have the hearts of people and not count them as dumb sheep who are led to slaughter. I thank You that they will not be hungry for filthy lucre but will care for the communities and surrounding cities. Bless many through the leadership that You currently have in place, dear Jesus. We thank You for it! In Jesus Christ's name, Amen.

5

PRAYING THROUGH FEAR

Another nugget to strongly consider in order to be successful in your intercession and prayer time is that one must make sure that they are not bound by the spirit of fear. Fear is an absolute barrier against freedom, healing, and full Deliverance. We must annihilate it and declare it not to be a part of our minds, spirits, and souls. During my time of deliverance, one thing that I didn't know that I had was a spirit of fear.

When God presented me with a new part of the spirit realm, I realized that I wasn't free of fear. Every hidden area of fear that was in my life surfaced during that time. This is why it is so important to allow the Lord to constantly deliver us and heal us in every area of our lives. We must lay down everything we thought we knew and come before Him as dear children. We must allow Him to overturn the pebble, the stone, the rock, the boulder, and anything else that may be hidden deep within our souls. What we cannot see on our own, we must give Jesus Christ access to bring us to a place of maturity to see. That includes the corridors of our hearts and minds to expose it so we can war efficiently. That said, one must be careful when saying to God that you desire to "see in the spirit" or asking God to take you to realms you've never experienced before. Let God "grow" you there. You may not be as ready as you think you are. Allow God to process you to your next level. To my surprise, I had a lot of work to do and a lot of submitting to God to do in order for Him to remove it.

If one wrestles with any kind of fear, they will not be able to kill the enemy in prayer. Fear is a playground for the enemy to play with the mind of the believer. Satan knows if a Christian states that he is afraid of anything, the Christian doesn't fully trust the Lord as they should. Proverbs 3:5 (KJV) states that we are to trust the Lord with all of our hearts and lean not to our own understanding but in all our ways to acknowledge the Lord, and He will direct our paths. With everything we do and everything we are, we have to trust God with our very lives. This will drive out fear because we choose to trust God, not fear. You can't be afraid and say that you trust God at the same time. You have to choose whom you are going to serve. The Bible states in Joshua 24:15, "And if it seem evil unto you to serve the Lord choose you this day whom ye will serve; whether the gods which your fathers served that were on the other side of the flood or the gods of the Amorites, in whose land ye dwell: but as for me and my house we will serve the Lord." We have to make a permanent choice in our hearts, minds, spirits, and souls as to whom we will serve. Will it be fear, or will it be God?

The demon of fear is already defeated by the power of God and the blood of Jesus Christ. One cannot pray scared. You have to know that the Bible declares that God has given us all power over the enemy, and nothing by any means can hurt, harm, or endanger you (Luke 10:19). Be reminded that the Word of God tells us that we have authority (permission and power from God) and that, in the name of Jesus Christ, the spirit of fear must bow. There is no need for you to fear when you know who is doing the work of deliverance and annihilation (Zechariah 4:6). The detailed prayer below will help you overcome and annihilate the spirit of fear, in Jesus's name.

❧

<u>Prayers that Annihilate the Spirit of Fear</u>

Dearest Jesus, thank You so much for giving me a portion of the Father, which is the Holy Spirit, to live inside of me. I love You for your loving kindness towards me, Father. 2 Timothy 1:7 declares that You haven't given me the spirit of fear but of love, power, and a sound mind. Father, I thank You that Your declarations concerning me are true, and I believe them. I thank You that fear is leaving me right now. All hidden fears—fear of the unknown, fear of the known, fear of failure, fear of the dark side, fear of deliverance, fear of trusting, and fear of dying—must leave me right now in Jesus Christ's name.

We break the covenant with all fear from the womb that may have transferred to us from our parents in Jesus Christ's name. I break with the hammer of God's generation of fear that has been released on my bloodline in Jesus Christ's name. I refuse to walk in and live in fear; I will be at peace in every area of my life in the name of Jesus Christ. I have authority over you fear, and I dismantle and disarm your ability to paralyze my destiny and purpose in the name of Jesus Christ. I dismantle, roast by fire, any feelings of insecurity or a sense of being emotionally over-whelmed in the name of Jesus Christ. I will not be paralyzed and will walk freely, as Your Word declares that I can in John 8:36. I am not bound by any demonic padlock that has been sent through or by the spirit of fear to paralyze me. I snatch the key of any demonic padlock back from the enemy in the name of Jesus Christ. I release myself from spiritual paralysis.

In You, Lord, I move, live, and have my being in Jesus Christ's name. I will go forward and conquer the land, all for

Your glory, in the name of Jesus Christ. I will not be afraid to move into whom You have called me to be in the name of Jesus Christ. My heart, mind, spirit, and soul will not be bound by any form of demonic paralysis induced by the spirit of fear in the name of Jesus Christ. I command my emotions to align with the Word of God, and I thank You, Father, that the spirit of fear will not make me cry, make wrong sporadic choices, lie, destroy relationships, or torment myself because I'm afraid. I will make sound decisions without being pressured by the spirit of fear, in the name of Jesus Christ. I will not be insecure about who You have called me to be as a believer in Christ Jesus because I fear people and their opinions. I will uniquely be myself and will not be moved to pursue accolades from anyone else to validate myself. I accept who You say that I am, and I will not be intimidated by the spirit of fear. I am not fearful of not being accepted, for I know that I have been accepted by You. I know that I am an heir with God and a joint heir with Jesus Christ, according to Romans 8:17. I am Your creation, and I know that I am beautifully and wonderfully made, according to Psalms 139:14. I receive and believe Your Word towards me,

Father. I thank You, Father, that Your Word tells me in Isaiah 43:1 not to fear, for You have redeemed me. Father, I thank You for redeeming me from the hand of the enemy and calling me by name. I thank You that I belong to You, and what the enemy tries will not work in Jesus's name. Lord, as You told Joshua to be courageous in Joshua 1:9, I, by choice, choose not to walk in fear but boldly be courageous and walk in power and authority. Father, I thank You that I will not be afraid of the unknown. I will be at peace in my heart, mind, spirit, and soul. I will trust You with what I don't know, can see, or feel. I will not tap into dark realms or spheres to find out what's going on in the unknown realm in order to know what will happen next because of fear. I will not fear the future, and Father, no matter what happens, I know that You have me in the palm of your hands.

Father, You are my protector. I trust what and whom You allow me to come into contact with, and I will not continue to be afraid of the unknown. Father, help me not to be afraid. I thank You, Lord, that my mind is sound, and I will not be afraid of what I see, sense, feel, or encounter in the spirit realm. I will not feel threatened by darkness and the spirit of fear.

I declare that no spirit, but the Spirit of the living God will rest on and in me, in Jesus's name. I will not be afraid of the angels of the Lord Jesus Christ. I will not be afraid of God and will only have a holy reverence for Him as Creator. Father, I thank You that I will not be afraid to dig deeper in prayer to encounter Your glory more. I will allow You to pour Yourself into me through and during prayer and intercession. I will not be afraid of retaliation from the enemy for doing Your will. We bind retaliation and remind it that we have authority over it in the name of Jesus Christ. Father, I will not be afraid of Satan and any of his demons or principalities. Satan is a forever defeated foe, and I will never defeat him whom my Father in Heaven has already defeated on Calvary's Cross in the name of Jesus Christ. Father, I praise You for the precious blood that was shed for me, and Your blood is a reminder to me and the devil of how great you are.

Father, I thank You that I am not afraid of the dark, darkness, or being alone. I am the salt of the earth, and a light that is set on a holy hill will shine for Your glory, according to Matthew 5:13. God, Your light in me shines brighter than any darkness that Satan will try to bring my way. I am free, and I will not allow the enemy to entangle my mind in darkness, in Jesus's name. The light of God in me will shine through any dark place or dark storm in Jesus's name, and I will not be afraid of the terror by night or the noisome pestilence by day, according to Psalms 91:3. I thank You, Lord, that Your Word declares in Psalms 27:1 that, "The LORD is my light and my salvation; whom shall I fear? The LORD is the strength of my life; of whom shall I be afraid?" You demon of fear, I see you and know you are only as big as I make you. I will not be afraid. I am taking my sanity, love, joy, and peace back in the name of Jesus Christ. I will not take your torment, as I know that the Word of God states in 1st John 4:18 that fear brings torment, but perfect love casts out fear. My love is made perfect in the Father, and I am no longer captive to you, fear, in the name of Jesus Christ. I command you, in the name of Jesus Christ, to shrink and disappear forever. Do not return to my life in Jesus's name.

Father, I thank You that Your Word declares in John 14:27, "Peace I leave with you, my peace I give unto you: not as the world giveth, give I unto you. Let not your heart be troubled, neither let it be afraid." I thank You, Lord, for Your peace in my heart, mind, spirit, and soul. I thank You, Lord, that Your peace keeps me from having anxiety attacks and panic attacks. I thank You, Lord, that I will not fear what men will try to do to me. I will not fear or panic about the economy or what danger befalls this nation. I will trust You, Lord, with my life. Lord, I will not fear and have anxiety attacks due to being overwhelmed by my job, such as being a mother or father to my children, a married spouse, or being overwhelmed with ministry. Father, Your Word tells me in 1 Peter 5:7 that I should cast my cares upon the Lord and that You care for me. Father, I choose to cast all of my fears upon You, knowing that You will destroy them with Your glory in the name of Jesus Christ.

Father, in the name of Jesus Christ, I thank You that I will not be afraid to be in a relationship due to previous bad relationships. I will not have a fear of loving my spouse with eros love. I will not fear loving my church family and leaders with agape love. I will not be afraid to love my family with storge love. I will open my heart and love again through the heart of the Father and with true discernment of the Holy Spirit. Father, I will not put good people in a bad category due to being afraid of being hurt again. Father, place a seal of Your blood upon my heart, mind, and spirit so that I will know how to love again genuinely and not be afraid of being hurt in the name of Jesus Christ. Lord, I trust You. Father, I thank You that I am fully free from the spirit of fear. I thank You that I have the anointing of Heaven to destroy, roast by fire, and suffocate any form of fear that has been assigned to me from Hell. I have power over you fear, and I render you helpless, powerless, and hopeless in the name of Jesus Christ, amen.

6

PRAYERS AGAINST THE SPIRIT OF UNBELIEF

Father God, in the name of Jesus, I thank You for faith. I thank You that I have the radical faith to destroy the enemy. I thank You that my faith pleases You, according to Hebrews 11:6. I thank You that my faith is so strong, Lord, that the gates of Hell shake and rattle in despair, pain, and anguish when I choose to trust You. Lord, I believe that you are the author and finisher of my faith, according to Hebrews 12:2. Lord, I know that if I believe what You said about me in Your Word with my entire heart, mind, spirit, and soul, You will come to my rescue in any situation. Lord, I chase the demon of unbelief away from me in the name of Jesus Christ. I break my covenant with it in Jesus Christ's name! I thank You, Lord, that every spirit of unbelief is totally annihilated by Your legal blood and no longer exists in my life or the lives of your people, in Jesus Christ's name.

Father, we know and understand that without faith, it is impossible to please You. Today, we arm ourselves with the shield of faith and utilize it to crush the head of unbelief in Jesus Christ's name. Unbelief, you have no place in my life, heart, mind, or spirit. I will please God by believing in His holy Word.

I command every demonic charm that has been projected into my belief system in the Lord Jesus Christ, my mind, or my life to be roasted by fire now in the name of Jesus Christ. Every demonic charm that Hell has projected into my mind to bind up my heart with demonic oppression to keep me from believing Your will for my life, implode right now in the name of Jesus Christ. We release fire on you at the root! May your demonic network assigned to frustrate my life be roasted by fire NOW, in Jesus Christ's name.

I will trust in the Lord! I will stand on the Word of God! I will not live in fear, and I will not prepare my heart and mind for failure. Everything that I touch will be prosperous in Jesus Christ's name. Father, I thank You that every demonic projection of unbelief sent to me by demonic chants and incantations, agents of Satan, word curses, lies, gossip, and deceit to stop me from believing that the Word of God is true is now destroyed by fire. Lord, we paralyze the tongue of the chanter and incantator in the name of Jesus Christ. We slice the tongue of the wicked one with the sword of the Spirit in Jesus Christ's name. We thank You, Lord, that we live and walk by faith, not by sight, according to 2 Corinthians 5:7. I thank You, Lord, that our faith is not absent and that we will believe You no matter what. Father, thank You for breaking the neck of every demonic unbelief system all over the world and that we, Your people, will believe, pray, and stand fast on what You told us in Your holy Word.

Father, Your Word declares that Satan is the father of all lies. We break the covenant with every demonic word of unbelief that Satan has whispered about our destinies and purposes. We declare Your truth and faith in our hearts and minds. We will believe in God and His infallible Word. We will not operate from a place of unbelief. Father, Your Word tells us that we are to pray and believe, in Mark 11:24. Father, I trust You with my life, and I will not walk in unbelief. You are the way, truth, and life, according to John 14:6, and I know that You will come through for Your people in Jesus Christ's name. Any trial that comes my way will not swallow me up but will be consumed by Your glory. Father, you are great, and I look for manifestation of your promises, not failure. In Jesus Christ's name, amen.

∾

Let's War and Win!

Ok, now that we have covered our atmosphere and pertinent things that are needed to prepare you and your atmosphere for spiritual warfare, it's time to deal with the mind, body, spirit, and soul. Let's war and win in Jesus Christ's name!

7

———

PRAYERS AGAINST MIND BLOCKAGE

When one is praying against mind blockage, there are many different elements that must be considered. Over the last two years, God has shown me the root cause of why many people commit suicide, are not able to complete various tasks that God has given them, have migraines and head pain, and suffer with the spirit of offense. All of the elements mentioned here, just to name a few, fall under the category of mind control or mind blockage. The culprit behind this is the spirit of the octopus, in conjunction with Jezebel.

We will focus on destroying the spirit of the octopus in this book. In this chapter, there are treasures of Heaven that the Father has released to me to expose Hell's plan to destroy each believer and mankind by simply tainting and blocking the gates of the mind. There are many demons that are sent from Hell to block, stop, and hinder each person on Earth from reaching their full potential and from being who God has made them to be. If you are writing a book, a business plan, or even a grant, there are demons that are sent directly from Hell to try to stop you. They will make you sleepy, lethargic, frustrated, or even block your mind from receiving Heavenly downloads to write it. If you are working on a project and need to go to another room to get something that is pertinent to you completing the project, the enemy will make you forget what they went into the room for. If you are trying to obey God and get on the correct path with exercising and eating healthy, there are demons from Hell that are released to make you extremely tired, keep you from going to the gym, make you forget to workout, or even make you crave the very thing that you are trying to walk away from. These are examples of how warfare starts in the mind first. The great news is that there is a way to escape.

The Bible states in 1 Corinthians 10:13, "No temptation has overtaken you except such as is common to man; but God is faithful, who will not allow you to be tempted beyond what you are able, but with the temptation will also make the way of escape, that you may be able to bear it." God will bring you out and give you your mind back if you simply pray. There are demonic spirits that are assigned to the lives of believers to control their minds and emotions. We must not be ignorant concerning Satanic devices if we plan on conquering our struggles in life on our way to Heaven.

We must acknowledge that the spirit realm is more real than the natural realm and not worry about people calling us "deep" or saying that "it doesn't take all of that." Beloved of God, it does "take all of that!" You are not deep or spooky, but you've learned that you must war in prayer and intercession to keep your mind in a place of peace and sanity. Never come down off the wall of intercession to compromise what God is allowing you to experience.

Live your life in a way where you are totally free from the opinions of others. Deliverance from people is the most beautiful thing ever! You are not crazy! Spiritual warfare is real! And those who would judge you for warring the way that you do are simply "too low." Meaning that they have chosen a life of mediocrity and complacency. The Bible states in Matthew 5:6,

"Blessed are those that thirst and hunger after righteousness for they shall be filled." If you are hungry, God will fill you with more of Him as you surrender to him more. The desperate the seek, the greater the pour from the Father. Just genuinely seek Him.

We are children of God! The Bible states that if we are risen with Christ, we will seek those things that are above (Colossians 3:1). If one chooses to descend downward dimensions, trying to explain the place that God has allowed them to ascend to or trying to fit in with people that were clearly left at ground level during their ascension, that intercessor will experience extreme warfare. Descending back into old habits is very dangerous. Stay free. Stay in the presence of God! Never compromise or down-play yourself because of the desire for accolades or approval from others. Going back and picking up people and things that God has brought you up and out of will cause all of the old demons to beat you up terribly. Will you descend to please people and not God? Yes, it will be hard and lonely. Yes, you will cry but always choose God. Never ever allow anyone to change your heart and mind about what God is saying to you and doing in your life. That is mind control and manipulation. Stay focused. The Kingdom of Heaven is at hand, and the time is now for you to stay free and continue to ascend to where God is! You will only find God in His glory!

8

SPIRIT OF THE OCTOPUS

This marine spirit is very subtle and cunning. This culprit is part of a very dark underworld kingdom that thrives on dysfunction and blocks the minds of every believer in Christ Jesus. In order to destroy it, one must aim for the heart of the octopus. The octopus has 3 hearts believe it or not, and it also has 9 brains. One in the main cavity of the head, one in each arm (2), and one in all six of each tentacle. This gives the octopus a total of 9 brains. The nine brains in operation allow the octopus to do multiple things individually at one time with one main goal in mind. That is, to destroy, eat, and consume the things they captured. Many spirits work as an arm of the octopus to destroy many of the believers of Jesus Christ. Each tentacle and each arm literally have a demonic mind of their own. Cutting off a tentacle or damaging other parts of this particular spirit's body will not destroy it. It has the power to regenerate (grow back) any part of its body.

The octopus has 3 hearts, which is a representation of a demonic falsehood. It's a false trinity. We must keep in mind that the devil is a mimicker and a copycat; he cannot create. This spirit is sent specifically to target the believers and bite them in the head to change their minds about the truth of the Word of God. If this spirit changes the mind or alters the minds of the believers in Christ Jesus, it will change the hearts of the believers and cause them to operate in error. This alone is a form of charismatic witchcraft. Remember, the Word of God tells us in Proverbs 4:23, "Guard your heart above all else, for it determines the course of your life." We are to guard our hearts from anything corrupt and demonic. Jesus Christ is the only one who should be at home in our hearts.

The spirit of the octopus is sent to detour believers in Christ Jesus from having a pure heart, twist things of God, and destroy pure, genuine love for the body of Christ. It is a very religious spirit that loves to attack many believers in Christ Jesus who serve in their local body at their church to cause them to not live a life of holiness and purity outside of the church. It is a falsehood. If we target all three of the heart cavities, it will instantly die.

In order to defeat this demonic spirit, we must pray with strategy. The octopus also has a very unique mouth and teeth. Its mouth is a crossbreed between a swordfish and a land bird, hybrid in form. The outer portion of its mouth is shaped like a very sharp beak, and the inside of its mouth is serrated like a very jagged sword. This allows the octopus to catch its prey, kill its prey, and destroy its prey quickly. The beak is as sharp as a razor blade, which allows the bite of the octopus to go deep into its prey with the first initial bite. Once bitten, it can then consume and devour its prey quickly with razor-sharp serrated teeth. One bite can lead to the death of its prey. We must make sure that we remain consistent in prayer in order to keep our discernment sharpened to be able to detect anything razor-sharp that the enemy tries to send into the life of believers in Christ Jesus.

The octopus typically camouflages itself in the shadows,

waiting for its prey to lose watch of its surroundings, and then pounces on the head of its prey. Biting it and devouring it.

This spirit has gone undetected for a very long time within the body of Christ, but now God is setting the captive free from this venomous demon. No longer will it be allowed to bite the head of the believer and release dark, venomous poison into the brain cavity of the children of God. No longer will it be allowed to walk around in our lives undetected because of its flexibility to hide in the cracks and crevices of our lives. God is breaking chains of toxic thoughts and relationships through sexual perversion and/or manipulative connections. No longer will God allow this spirit to continue to harm the people of God! Let's attack this spirit in prayer and shut down its assignment over your life.

Below are prayers that will show you how to fight against the attacks of Satan on the brain through the spirit of the octopus and your emotions to keep you from walking on purpose. Let's war and win in Jesus Christ's name! Amen!

<u>Prayer against the Spirit of the Octopus | Mind Control</u>

Father, we thank You that Your Word declares that whom the Son sets free is free indeed. We thank You that when we call upon You for deliverance, You always come to our rescue. Father, today, we take authority over the spirit of the octopus in the name of Jesus Christ. Father, today we roast by fire every marine spirit sent on assignment to destroy our destinies and our purpose on this earth in the name of Jesus Christ. Father, we thank You that the spirit of the octopus is destroyed from the root in the name of Jesus Christ. We banish him from our homes, lives, bodies, families, and friends in the name of Jesus Christ.

Octopus, we break the covenant with you. You have no

authority over us, in the name of Jesus Christ. Father, we thank You that the heart of the octopus is destroyed with the hammer of God and the sword of the Spirit in the name of Jesus Christ. We snatch the hearts of the octopus out of his chest cavity, and we command it to be roasted by fire now in the name of Jesus Christ. We thank You for killing the octopus, oh God, in the name of Jesus Christ!

Father, now that we have removed the heart of the octopus, we strategically cut off every tentacle of the octopus in the name of Jesus Christ. We speak to every nerve ending and every cell of the tentacle and command it to completely die and not remain operable in the name of Jesus Christ. Do not regenerate! Die in Jesus Christ's name! Thank You, Father, for destroying every demonic connection acquired over our lives while the octopus was alive in our lives in the name of Jesus Christ. We thank You that every demonic tentacle that built strong demonic relationships, connections, friendships, soul ties, addictions, and anything that isn't of You, Father, is broken now in the name of Jesus Christ.

Father, we break covenant with demonic churches, demonic alliances, sororities, fraternities, masonic and eastern star alliances, occultic practices, religious teaching, demonic family members, familiar spirits, self-sabotage, and any hidden stronghold over our lives, known and unknown, in the name of Jesus Christ. Anything affiliated with the tentacle or arm of the octopus that was in our lives, we roast you by fire now in the name of Jesus Christ. We know the law of God. We believe in the power of God! You false trinity, be destroyed at the root in the name of Jesus Christ! We've broken the covenant with you and your subgroupings in the name of Jesus Christ.

Father, we will no longer walk in defeat because of this spirit. Thank You for setting us free in the name of Jesus Christ! You are worthy, oh God!

We break the covenant with demonic habits formed in our

lives while we were under the demonic control of the octopus that caused us to miss the wind of Your Spirit blowing in our lives in the name of Jesus Christ. Father, we break covenant with old boyfriends, old girlfriends, ex-husbands, and ex-wives with lesbian and homosexual relationships in the name of Jesus Christ. Every soul tie be roasted by fire now! Every demon that transferred to us from old tentacles, Father, we renounce and break the covenant with it in the name of Jesus Christ.

Jesus Christ, we choose You! Father, we destroy by fire every spirit of perversion that entered our lives while we were attached to the spirit of the octopus. You demonic tentacle that carried the spirit of incubus and succubus to hinder us from purpose, your time is up now in the name of Jesus Christ. We divorce you in the spirit realm. We roast your demonic marriage certificates with fire and remove our names from the wicked altars of the marine kingdom. You cannot have us! We belong to Jesus Christ! You will not win; we belong to Jesus Christ! We break your demonic flesh desire of masturbation over our lives in the name of Jesus Christ. Our hands were created to worship the Lord and bring good to the land in the name of Jesus Christ. We are creatives, not masturbators. We are inventors, not masturbators. We will lay hands on the sick, and they will recover in the name of Jesus Christ. We will not fondle ourselves, and dearest Jesus, we ask that You kill our flesh. Take the desire away from us to masturbate. Cover the gates of our minds with Your blood. We will not have sexual fantasies, but Your Word, oh God, we will meditate on both day and night in the name of Jesus Christ, Amen! We break the covenant with the tentacles of pornography, anal sex, couple swinging, adultery, fornication, and orgies. We break the covenant with the tentacle of bestiality and anything that is perverted that may have entered our lives while the spirit of octopus was in operation.

Father, we repent of things that we did out of ignorance and things that have become open doors of torment from the enemy in our lives. Father, forgive us for bringing the tentacle of sexual toys into our marriages, homes, and bedrooms in the name of Jesus Christ. Father, forgive us for exposing our children to any form of pornography, any form of perversion, or any form of anything that was outside of your will. Father, break any form of homosexuality that may have entered our lives while we were under the influence of this demon spirit in the name of Jesus Christ. We thank You for breaking it in Jesus Christ's name.

Father, we thank You for breaking the residue of mind control off of us that the spirit of the octopus had us under while it was alive, in the name of Jesus Christ. Father, You are good to us, and Your mercy endures forever. Thank You for finding us right where we were and for not leaving us to die under the spell and manipulation of the spirit of the octopus. Hallelujah.

Father, thank You for breaking clairvoyance out of our lives. Thank You for destroying every 3rd eye in the name of Jesus Christ. Thank You, Lord, for setting us free from familiar spirits that entered our lives through the spirit of the octopus in the name of Jesus Christ.

Father, thank You for breaking the shackles and chains off our minds from the spirit of the octopus that will keep us from reading Your Word and from praying in the name of Jesus Christ. Father, I thank You that we enjoy reading and studying Your Word. I thank You that we crave Your presence and prayer in the name of Jesus Christ. Thank You, oh God! Thank You for destroying the tentacles that have kept us from fasting and that cause us to be distracted and not perform our best at daily tasks in the name of Jesus Christ.

We declare and decree that we can take care of our families, be successful performers in our jobs, and perform exceptionally well within the marketplace and our homes. Father, I thank You that we are good parents, great children, and great husbands and wives. I thank You that we are good spiritual children and have submitted to leadership in the name of Jesus Christ. I thank You that we are no longer under the influence of the octopus, in the name of Jesus Christ. I thank You that it's done in the name of Jesus Christ, amen!

Father, thank You for removing the dark, venomous ink from our eyes that the octopus released over our lives while he was alive. Father, thank You for causing us to see and comprehend things clearly in the name of Jesus Christ. Thank You, Lord, for moving the dark veil of being judgmental away from our lives in the name of Jesus Christ. Father, thank You for removing the dark, poisonous venom of jealousy from our lives in the name of Jesus Christ. Father, we remove the beak of the octopus from the gates of our minds in the name of Jesus Christ. Dear Lord, You are good to us, and Your mercy endures forever. Hallelujah!

We command every uncommon headache that is associated with the spirit of the octopus be removed now in the name of Jesus Christ. Blood pressure be regulated back to normalcy in the name of Jesus Christ. A1C be aligned to the right number in the name of Jesus Christ. Father, I rid our bodies of all toxins that the spirit of the octopus injected into our bloodstream in the name of Jesus Christ. We drive out all heavy carbon deposits within our bloodstreams sent to release PCOS in the name of Jesus Christ. We drive out all devastation to the male and female genitals sent by the octopus in the name of Jesus Christ. We destroy and annihilate infertility in any form in the name of Jesus Christ. We are producers. We are birthers in the spirit and the natural, in the name of Jesus Christ. We break the covenant with you, octopus. You have no power over us or our destinies in the name of Jesus Christ. Father, I thank You that healing is our portion in the name of Jesus Christ. It is so, in Jesus's name, amen!

I thank You that the octopus will not wrap itself around me to control my mind and emotions in the name of Jesus Christ. Fire of God, cover our minds, bodies, spirits, and souls. Dearest Jesus, make us infernos for you! Fire of God, consume us! Make us walking fires for the Lord. Set us ablaze! Make us hot for God so that nothing or no one will be able to control or manipulate us, Father, in the name of Jesus Christ.

Father, Your Word declares in Philippians 2:5, "Let this mind be in you, which was also in Christ Jesus." Father, today we take on Your mind and heart for our lives. Father, we thank You that no spirit, but the Spirit of the living God will rest, rule, and abide over our lives in the name of Jesus Christ. Father, we thank You that no weapon formed against our minds will prosper. Father, we thank You that the beak of the octopus that was left embedded in our heads after we've destroyed it is gently removed now in the name of Jesus Christ.

Every place in our minds that the beak of the octopus sank into, we declare healing over it now in the name of Jesus Christ. We destroy the plan of the octopus to try to break our minds in the name of Jesus Christ. Lord, I declare and decree that we have sound minds full of life and vitality in the name of Jesus Christ. We come against all demonic hits that have been put out on our lives from Hell in the name of Jesus Christ. We have a sound mind! Be gone from us in the name of Jesus Christ. Demonic headaches, migraines, and demonic venom that are sent to confuse and fog the human mind, be roasted now by the fire of God in the name of Jesus Christ.

Father, we thank You that You are God of Light and not of Darkness, and today, in the name of Jesus Christ, we take authority over every migraine spirit that is in operation as a tentacle from the octopus in the name of Jesus Christ. We will not have to take medication for headaches or migraines in the name of Jesus Christ. We will not have to go see specialists because of migraines and uncommon headaches in the name of Jesus Christ. We will not have seizures, we will not have aneurysms, and we will not have portions of our brain fried. We thank You that it is done in the name of Jesus Christ. Father, Your Word declares in Proverbs 3:24, "When you lie down, you will not be afraid; when you lie down, your sleep will be sweet."

Father, in the name of Jesus Christ, we come against the spirit of nightmares in the name of Jesus Christ. Residue of fear imparted to us by the spirit of the octopus, you are a foul liar! Make your exit now and leave! Never return. Leave the dreams of children! Leave the dreams of adults! Pack your bags and go! Do not return in the name of Jesus Christ. We will have restful sleep, not tormented sleep, in the name of Jesus Christ! Amen!

We cover the gates of our minds with the legal blood of Jesus Christ while we are asleep, in the name of Jesus Christ. We release the defenders of the Faith to stand guard at the gates of our minds with their swords, shields, and wings dipped in the legal blood of Jesus Christ as we rest. Father, I thank You that when we lay down to sleep at night, You protect us in the name of Jesus Christ.

We declare peace over the gates of our minds while we rest in the name of Jesus Christ. We declare love in the atmosphere while we rest in the name of Jesus Christ. Father, we thank You that You have not given us the spirit of fear but of love, power, and a sound mind. Father, we thank You that when we lie down to sleep, our sleep will be sweet. No spirit of torture will come in the night to attack the gates of our minds. Our dreams will not be blocked or affected by the tentacle of the octopus (nightmare/mind blockage) in the name of Jesus Christ. We release the angels of the Lord to come and to be on every wall, shoulder to shoulder, foot to foot, wing to wing, and ankle to ankle, to cover the atmosphere of our bedrooms and our very home in the name of Jesus Christ. We release you to fight and annihilate anything that is not like the Father in the name of Jesus Christ, amen!

Father, we thank You that we will hear Your voice while we are asleep. We thank You that the gates of our minds are filled with truth, Your Word, joy, and Your legal blood in the name of Jesus Christ. Father, we thank You that every wicked imagination that tries to attack us in our sleep is cast down in the name of Jesus Christ. We are completely covered by Your blood in Jesus Christ, amen. Father, thank You that all the venom that was released from the octopus over the gates of our minds to block our dreams is removed now in the name of Jesus Christ. Father, I thank You that we see and hear clearly from You in our most vulnerable time of the night, our sleep. Father, I thank You for continuing to show us Your mysteries, love, and a little piece of Heaven, as You have always done while we are resting in the name of Jesus Christ.

Father, thank You for breaking every ounce of mental confusion that the spirit of octopus released over our lives in the name of Jesus Christ. Father, Your Word declares in 1st Corinthians 14:33 (KJV), "For God is not the author of confusion, but of peace, as in all churches of the saints." Father, we understand that where there is confusion, there is no God. Father, we thank You for breaking the confusion from the minds of Your people in the name of Jesus Christ. Father, we thank You for breaking the confusion off of the lives of those whom we have come in contact within the name of Jesus Christ. Father, we ask that You forgive us for anything that may have been transferred to anyone while we were under the influence, demonic possession, and oppression of the spirit of the octopus in the name of Jesus Christ.

Father, as You have set us free, set those that are connected to us free as well, in the name of Jesus Christ, and we thank You that is done in Jesus's name, amen. Father, thank You in the name of Jesus Christ that all shortness of breath in our physical bodies that the spirit of the octopus has caused to attack our lungs, our chest cavity, and our bodies is destroyed now in the name of Jesus Christ. Father, we thank You that Your Ruah is our portion now in the name of Jesus Christ.

We thank You, Father, for destroying every attack of asthma, every attack of swollen lymph nodes, every attack on our tonsils, and every attack on our airway passages, in Jesus's name. Father, we thank You that we are healed in the name of Jesus Christ. We thank You, Lord, that the tentacles of the octopus are no longer living to choke us, strangle us, and make us feel like we do not have a voice and that we can't worship You in the beauty of holiness. Father, we thank You that everything that the spirit of the octopus sent to choke out of us is released back upon him now in the name of Jesus Christ. Father, we thank You for restoring our worship. Father, we thank You for restoring our love, joy, and peace in the name of Jesus Christ. Father, we thank You for restoring the passion for ministry and the passion to do the work of the evangelist in the name of Jesus Christ.

Father, we thank You for restoring the joy of our salvation in the name of Jesus Christ. Father, You are good, and Your mercy endures forever. Thank you, God, that you did not allow the spirit of the octopus to destroy us and kill us. We thank You for Your love for us in Jesus's name. Thank You, Father, for causing us to breathe again in You! You are life! In Jesus Christ's name, amen!

Father, we thank You for revealing these hidden problems of the octopus in our lives in the name of Jesus Christ. We thank You, Father, that all that the octopus has hidden in our lives and even in our bloodline is broken in the name of Jesus Christ. Father, roast by fire every demonic river, stream, ocean, lake, and river that this spirit has hidden in the name of Jesus Christ. Every place in our lives, Father, that the spirit of octopus has hidden and camouflaged itself in plain sight in our lives, may Your light shine in that place in the name of Jesus Christ. May Your light destroy its nocturnal habitation and eyesight in the name of Jesus Christ.

Father, our hearts desire to please You and to always do the right thing. We give You free rein to explore the gates of our soul and to set us free. Do surgery within us. Father, we desire You, not a marine spirit, to reign over our lives in the name of Jesus

Christ. Father, we desire freedom, not bondage. Father, we desire to be full of Your love, grace, mercy, and joy in the name of Jesus Christ. Father, in every part of our lives that the spirit of octopus has camouflaged itself into that, has become normal to us, we ask that You expose it and remove it in the name of Jesus Christ. Father, we ask You to break the wrist of the octopus that tries to hold us in captivity while in hiding. Father, we smoke out every octopus that is hiding in our lives in the name of Jesus Christ. Father, we thank You that the octopus will no longer manipulate us to be something that we're not in the name of Jesus Christ. Father, we thank You that we will not be mimickers but that we will be creatives on earth and do just what You call us to do in the name of Jesus Christ.

We thank You, Lord, that every part of us looks like You, smells like You, and looks like You in the name of Jesus Christ. Father, we thank You. We shine with the light of Christ, according to Matthew 5 and 16. Father, we will not hide ourselves and the anointing that You put on the inside of us for the satisfaction of the others around us. We will walk in the light in order to draw others to You in the name of Jesus Christ! Father, we thank You that You are the prince of peace and have given us Your peace in the name of Jesus Christ. We thank You that we will no longer be manipulated by the spirit of the octopus and try to be something that You have not called us to be in the name of Jesus Christ.

Father, Your Word declares in Psalms 139:14, "I am fearfully and wonderfully made." Father, I thank You for making every-thing about me beautiful, and I have no need to be controlled by the spirit of the octopus in the name of Jesus Christ. Thank You for removing the residue of mind control from our lives in the name of Jesus Christ. Octopus, you failed again! My mind belongs to Christ, not you! Be gone from me in the name of Jesus Christ! Amen!

Father, I thank You for destroying every familiar spirit that works in conjunction with the spirit of the octopus through witchcraft in the name of Jesus Christ. Father, I thank You that every ounce of my life that has been recorded through the memory bank of the spirit of octopus is broken now in the name of Jesus Christ. I command the brain of the octopus that's holding that memory to implode now in the name of Jesus Christ! Father, I thank You that the pattern of my life that the octopus has recorded and shared in conjunction with familiar spirits to hinder, stop, and block my life from prospering and moving forward in the things of God is broken now by the legal blood of Jesus Christ.

Father, I thank You that every tentacle of the octopus is roasted by fire in the name of Jesus Christ. I thank You that every demonic brain and mind that works in conjunction with the tentacles of the octopus is destroyed now by the fire of God. Father, I thank You that you are hearing the cries of your children even now, in the name of Jesus Christ. Break demonic oppression. Break it, God, in the name of Jesus Christ. Father, I thank You that after today, we, as the children of God, will live free in our minds because we have destroyed every demonic heart of the octopus, which causes the remainder of its body to be destroyed and unable to regenerate. Father, I thank You that old mindsets will not regenerate. Father, thank You that old desires and relationships will not be rekindled or regenerated in our lives.

Father, we thank You that every demonic stronghold that is working in conjunction with the arm or the tentacle of the octopus is released from me right now in Jesus Christ's name. I am free in my mind. I am free in my heart. I am free to think rationally about the things of God in the name of Jesus Christ. I am no longer under the spell or mind control of the spirit of the octopus, in the name of Jesus Christ.

Father, thank You for pulling me from the depths of the ocean out of the clutches of the spirit of the octopus and giving me my mind back in the name of Jesus Christ. Father, I thank You for your love. Thank you for revealing what was wrong with me, in the name of Jesus Christ. Father, thank You for showing me that there is nothing wrong with me and that I am not incompetent. I thank You that I can do all things through Christ who strengthens me, and Father, I thank You that all pain in my head, arms, legs, body, and feet, even in my genital area, is completely healed in the name of Jesus Christ. Jesus, You are Lord, and we thank You, amen.

9

COVERING THE GATES OF THE MIND

Now that we've destroyed the spirit of the octopus, let's look at the human mind through a different set of lenses. The human mind is an absolutely amazing thing that God created. The chart below will allow you to understand why it's important for our brain and mind to function according to the Word of God and nothing else. Let's take our minds, bodies, spirits, and souls back, all for the glory of God in the name of Jesus Christ!

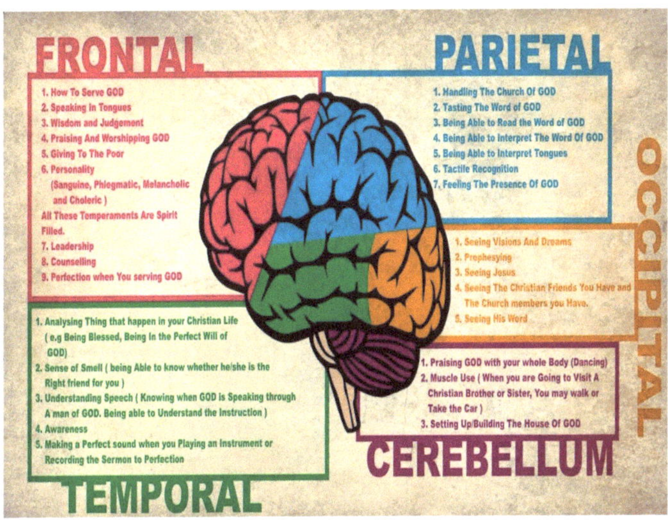

Father God, in the name of Jesus Christ, I thank You that Your Word declares in Philippians 2:5, "Let this mind be in me that is also in Christ Jesus." I thank You that my mind and thought patterns belong to You. I thank You that You have given me a sound mind and that I think rationally and clearly. I thank You that the gates of my mind are covered in the legal blood of Jesus Christ and that warring angels stand on guard, protecting my mind from all demonic attacks or projections from the wicked one. I thank You, Lord, that my mind has been bought with the price of the precious blood of Jesus Christ and that there are no refunds on my mind. I thank You, Lord, that every part of my brain that controls the gates of my mind is covered in the blood of Jesus Christ. I thank You that the frontal, parietal, temporal, cerebellum, and occipital parts of my brain and mind are covered in the blood of Jesus Christ. I thank You, Lord, that every demonic mind blocker or demonic mind controller sent from Hell to block me or control me is roasted by fire right now in the name of Jesus Christ. I declare and decree that I will be able to read, write, think, and speak clearly in the name of Jesus Christ.

Mind blockage, you demon, you will not make me forget sentences. Mind blockage, you demon, you will not make me forget where I left items in my house. Mind blockage, you demon, you will not make me forget what I walked into a room for in the name of Jesus Christ. Mind blockage, you will not make me block out past or current pain and cause me not to remember traumatic experiences that I've gone through to prevent me from obtaining my deliverance. Healing is my portion! You demon of mind blockage, you will not stop me from remembering what God's love for me feels like and make me not accept the love of God and His people. Be gone from me, mind blockage. You are powerless. I take my mind back. My mind belongs to God, and it will not be clogged, stopped, or blocked in the name of Jesus Christ. My mind is a funnel for Heaven to think and flow through. God will utilize my mind for His glory in the name of Jesus Christ. I will not have a schizophrenic mind in the name of Jesus Christ. I think with sanity and clarity in the name of Jesus Christ.

You demon of mind blockage that tells me that I am crazy and mentally insane, I renounce you right now in the name of Jesus Christ. My mind and brain are both filled with the blood of Jesus Christ. My mind and brain are fully redeemed by the cross, and I am free indeed. Oh yes!

Frontal Lobe

F ather, I thank You that the frontal lobe of my brain is fully healed, delivered, and set free from any demonic oppression in the name of Jesus Christ. I thank You, dear Lord, that every demon that tries to strip my desire to serve the Lord is sliced with the sword of the Spirit right now in the name of Jesus Christ.

Father, Your Word tells me to serve the Lord with gladness in Psalms 100:2. I will be glad to serve in the house of the Lord, and I will be glad to serve You, dear Jesus, in my home. I will be glad to serve You in my local community and even on my job. Lord, everything that I do, I will do it unto You, as Your Word instructs me to do so in 1 Corinthians 10:31. Lord, I thank You that the demon of mind blockage will not block my ability to speak in tongues. Lord, You have instructed us, Your people, in Jude 1:20, to build ourselves up in the most holy faith by praying in the Holy Spirit. I thank You that every demon that tries to tie up my tongue will die now in the name of Jesus Christ. I command my tongue to be loosed now, in the name of Jesus Christ. I will not only speak in tongues, but my mind is free from all sorts of mind blockages that try to block the flow from Heaven for the interpretation of tongues.

I thank You, Lord, that every demonic cord that wraps my tongue is loosed now in the name of Jesus Christ. I will not be blocked or bound in my mind, brain, heart, or spirit to release the blessings of the Lord over my life, the lives of my loved ones, and this world. Lord, Your Word declares in Matthew 12:34 that out of the abundance of the heart, the mouth speaks. Lord, I thank You that my mind is not blocked, whereas I can't hear what You are saying to me for the people, and I am not able to interpret the prophetic Word of the Lord that comes through speaking in tongues. I declare my tongue loose right now in the name of Jesus Christ!

Lord, as I continue to pray over and for the frontal lobe of my brain and mind, I thank You that I have wisdom and judge wisely. Lord, You told us in James 1:5: "If any of you lack wisdom, let him ask of God, that giveth to all men liberally, and upbraideth not; and it shall be given him." I thank You, Lord, that we have your wisdom, love, and grace. I thank You that we are not blocked by any demonic influence or power from making wise connections and decisions. Jesus, thank You for giving me the liberal wisdom to choose to serve you and fight against anything that isn't of the kingdom of God. I thank You, Lord, that Your Word declares in Psalm 111:10 (NIV) that "the fear of the LORD is the beginning of wisdom; all who follow his precepts have good understanding. To him belongs eternal praise." Lord, I thank You that I am not blocked in my mind or brain from having reverence and the fear of the Lord to obtain His wisdom. I thank You, Lord, that demonic fear will not replace the pure fear of God, and I will move freely in the wisdom of God in the name of Jesus Christ.

Dear Jesus, I thank You that I am not blocked from seeing Your Children as You see them. Lord, Your Word tells us in Matthew 7:1, "Judge not, that ye be not judged." I thank You, Lord, that I will not judge Your people based on the perceptions or opinions of others. I thank You, Lord, that every person I meet will receive Your love and not judgment from me. I thank You, Lord, that I will not be blocked by mind blockage to hold people in a spiritual prison due to rumors, lies, and false perceptions.

I thank You, Lord, that my mind is clear and open to hearing instructions from Heaven regarding anyone I encounter.

Angels of the Lord, come now and destroy the spirit of mind blockage that may try to make me operate in pride and not receive God's wisdom for His people as He would receive them in the name of Jesus Christ. Lord, thank You for unclogging and unblocking my mind in the name of Jesus Christ.

Father, I thank You because my mind is free to praise you. I thank You, Lord, that the enemy can't stop or block my praise. You demon of Thaddeus that comes to block and hinder me from praise and worship, I cut your head off in the name of Jesus Christ. I paralyze your tongue. I command your heart to fail in the name of Jesus Christ. I command the very breath that you use to breathe out demonic venom into the mind cavity to block prophetic worshipers and cause them to suddenly and permanently stop and fail right now in the name of Jesus Christ. My mind will not be blocked, and I will sing, dance, create, and flow prophetically in the name of Jesus Christ.

Dear Jesus, I thank You that the Word commands me to bless You at all times in Psalms 34:1. I am free, you demon of mind blockage. I will bless the name of the Lord in praise and worship. The lifting up of my hands, the moving of my feet, and the prophetic song of the Lord will flow from and out of me in the name of Jesus Christ. I will be able to make a joyful noise to the Lord. I will bring the Father glory on earth in the name of Jesus. I take the blood of Jesus Christ and saturate the demon that tries to block me in my mind from lifting the name of Jesus Christ. Choke on the blood of Jesus Christ. The Word of God tells me that if I lift the name of the Lord, He will draw all men to Himself, according to John 12:32. I am aware of your diabolical schemes, and I understand that if I praise God freely in my mind, it has the power to set others around me free. Father, I thank You that the demon of mind blockage that was sent by Satan to block my praise and worship has been annihilated in the name of Jesus Christ. And it is so!

Father, I thank You that I do not have a mental block in my mind about serving and giving to the poor. I thank You, Father, that Your Word declares that the poor will always be with us, according to Matthew 14:7. Lord, I thank You that any demonic blockage in my mind that is sent from Hell to make me feel like I am being used or that I have too much compassion to help the poor in spirit or the natural world is totally destroyed and dismantled right now in the name of Jesus Christ. Lord, thank You for giving me seed to sow to give to the poor. My mind is open to sowing seeds to those in need. My mind is open to sowing into ministry, my children, my home, and my leaders. My mind is not blocked from giving to those who hurt me out of obedience. I will obey with a pure heart, mind, and conscience in the name of Jesus Christ.

Lord, I thank You that my true personality is not blocked by any demonic force. Lord, I thank You that my true personality, whether it is sanguine, phlegmatic, melancholic, or choleric, is aligned with the Word of God. I will not be like a whirlwind, blown to and fro in my mind, and all over the place. I thank You, Lord, that the components of my mind are spirit-filled and not blocked with pain, anguish, frustration, and anger, in Jesus Christ's name.

I thank You, Lord, for submitting to your leadership, counseling, and the perfecting of the gifts that You have given me. I thank You, dear Jesus, that Satan and all of his demons are defeated. I thank You that I have power over the spirit of rebellion; I do not have an unteachable spirit, and I will not use my gifts from a dark realm. Lord, I thank You that I will not put up a mental block to my leadership, spouse, manager, or anyone in leadership in reference to obeying those that You have put over me. Your Word tells me, Lord, to obey those who have rule over me, according to Hebrews 13:7. You demon of rebellion, I rebuke you and renounce you in the name of Jesus Christ. I will not rebel, as rebellion is a sin of witchcraft, according to 1 Samuel 15:23. I will open my mind to obeying God's Word and be happy about it in the name of Jesus Christ.

Temporal

Lord, I thank You that the temporal part of my brain is covered with your blood, in the name of Jesus Christ. I thank you for sharp discernment and spiritual eyesight. I thank you that I can accurately decipher between light and darkness in the name of Jesus Christ. We release the fire of God against every demonic spirit that have been sent on assignment to stop us from getting to our purpose and walking in our destiny in the name of Jesus Christ. We remove every dark veil away from our spiritual eye gates and we command the light of Christ to be our portion forever in the name of Jesus Christ. Lord, we will always give You glory. Father you are all-powerful as your word states in Psalms 62:11.

Today we give you what is due to you in the name of Jesus Christ! Lord, Your Word declares in James 1:17, "Every good gift, every perfect gift, comes from above. These gifts come down from the Father, the creator of the Heavenly lights, in whose character there is no change at all." I thank You that I will not be bound in my mind by thinking that I create my own blessings and that I am my own deliverer. I understand that without You, dear Jesus, I am nothing. I submit my mind to You and ask You, dear Lord, to help me remain humble and at Your feet. Help me to remember that I did not bring myself out of bondage. Lord, Your Word tells us in 2 Corinthians 2:11 that "You will not have us ignorant concerning Satan's devices."

I thank You, Lord, that every spirit of deception that tries to block the temporal part of my mind or brain is destroyed now in the name of Jesus. Lord, I thank You that I will be able to fully discern the company that I keep. I thank You, dear Jesus, that I can smell Hell's demonic smoke before it gets to me. I thank You that I am able to detect by the Holy Spirit whether anyone I am connected to is in sync with You. I thank You, Lord, that I will be able to decipher between truth, manipulation, and deceit that may come from someone who thinks I am spiritually blind. Lord, I thank You that I have the power over the deception that will try to block my mind and keep me from hearing the true voice of God.

I thank You that the temporal lobe of my brain is filled with Your Holy Spirit in the name of Jesus Christ. I am aware, alert, and awakened to Your Spirit, oh God, and no demon of mind blockage will infiltrate me or stop me from being whole in Jesus's name. Satan, be bound in the name of Jesus! Hallelujah!

Parietal

Father, I thank You that the parietal part of my brain and mind is covered in your precious blood in the name of Jesus Christ. I thank You, Lord, that I have not put up a mental blockage against the saints of God and that I will love them with all purity, honesty, and genuineness in the name of Jesus Christ. I renounce all old church hurt and pain that will cause me to not treat God's people rightly in the name of Jesus Christ. I thank You, Lord, for the ability to teach, lead, train, push, and birth God's people with a pure heart, all for Your glory. My mind functions well! I am coherent and very intelligent.

I break the covenant with every curse spoken over my life by my family members, myself, or managers who declared that I will never be who You designed me to be. Father, Your Word declares in Philippians 4:13 (KJV) that I can do all things through Christ who strengthens me. Father, I was created to worship You, and I was born to win. Hallelujah!

Father, we thank You that we are your church, and we understand that if we mistreat one another, we are mistreating the body of Christ. Father, Your Word tells us in John 13:34 (KJV) that we are to love one another. I come against any mind blockage in the parietal lobe of my brain in the name of Jesus Christ. Nothing or no one will keep me from loving the believers in Christ Jesus and the nonbelievers in Christ Jesus. I thank You, Lord, for Your pure love, and I vow that I will handle Your people with care in the name of Jesus Christ.

Thank You, Father, that Your love will spill out on the people of God through our lives in the name of Jesus Christ. Father,

Your Word tells us in Psalms 34:8 that we are to taste and see that You are good. Lord, I thank You that You are sweeter than honey in a honeycomb. Lord, I thank You that I have power over every demonic spirit that would try to steal my time of searching and reading the holy scriptures in the name of Jesus Christ. Lord, You told me in 2 Timothy 2:15 to study to show myself approved, a worker who need not be ashamed but rightfully divide the Word of truth.

Lord, I thank You that every demon that attaches itself to my mind and blocks my mind from reading, studying, dividing, and interpreting the Word of God is now bound by the blood of Jesus Christ. Lord, I thank You that I have a strong Bible study life and that I have a love for the Word of God in the name of Jesus. Lord, Your Word tells us in 1 Corinthians 14:27 that we should speak in our Heavenly language and are to speak in tongues unashamedly often.

I dismantle and disarm every spirit and agent of Satan that has attacked my mouth and tongue in the name of Jesus Christ. I thank You that my tongue is that of a ready writer, according to Psalms 45:1. Father, as You are speaking through me, my tongue is a pen that will create truth, healing, and deliverance on earth in the name of Jesus Christ. I thank You that when I speak in tongues, I bring You glory in the earth, I build myself up in the Spirit, and I tear down Satan's dark kingdom.

Father, I command every evil demon from the pit of Hell to return to its dungeon and report back to Satan that they have failed on their assignment for me in the name of Jesus Christ. I thank You, Lord, that my tongue is loose. I can prophetically pray in tongues and declare blessings and the deliverances of God to hit the earth in the name of Jesus Christ. I thank You, Lord, for giving me the gift of tongues and that when I pray, I slay demons, dragons, and any dark entity from Hell in the name of Jesus Christ. I thank You, Lord, that I have tongues of fire that were released to me on the day of Pentecost. I thank You, Lord, that when I pray, demons run and flee because of Your power and fire that comes out of my mouth in the name of Jesus Christ. I thank You, Lord, that I am a creator with my mouth and that when I speak, demons submit to your power in the name of Jesus Christ.

Father, I thank You that my mind isn't blocked from remaining tactile with the people of God. I thank You, Father, that as You were touched by the infirmities of Your people, I will spiritually be able to feel, sense, know, and discern the hearts of Your people through Your Holy Spirit. I thank You, dearest Jesus, that I know that I am Your beloved and that I am able to feel Your presence with me. Father, I thank You that I am not moved by emotionalism but by the Spirit of God. Every demon sent to block my mind from being open to the Spirit of God touching me, be roasted by holy fire now in Jesus Christ's name. Father, I thank You that, as I worship You, the parietal part of my brain is wide open to receiving Your absolute love for me. I will love You as much as You love me. I enjoy Your presence, and I will dwell in the house of the Lord all the days of my life. In the name of Jesus Christ, amen!

<u>Occipital</u>

Father, I thank You that the occipital lobe of my brain is covered by the legal blood of Jesus Christ. Father, Your Word declares in Matthew 6:22–23, "The eye is the lamp of the body. If your eyes are healthy, your whole body will be full of light. But if your eyes are unhealthy, your whole body will be full of darkness. If then the light within you is darkness, how great is that darkness!" Father, I thank You that my eyes are healthy and whole. I thank You that I see You as the Lord and Savior of my life. I thank You that I have the ability to use the lens of Heaven to be able to discern that which is of You and that which isn't.

Father, I thank You that my eyes are purified and sanctified for Your use. I thank You, Lord, that our eyes are not covered by a dark veil from Hell. Lord, I thank You for destroying every queen cobra snake sent from Hell to stop and block my dreams, visions, and the true voice of God flowing out of me. Father, cover us while we are asleep. Let nothing attack us unknowingly in our dreams or visions. Let knowledge put a demonic barrier over our eyes.

Father, I thank You that Your Word declares in Psalms 34:15, "The eyes of the LORD are on the righteous, and his ears are attentive to their cry." I thank You, Lord, that I will see everything that You have destined me to see in part so that I may prophesy in part.

Father, I thank You for the occipital lobe of my brain. I thank you that I can prophesy accurately. I declare and decree that as I pray and seek Your face for Your people, you will allow me to see through Your eyes. Father, we close every clairvoyant 3rd eye that will try to connect to us and look through our eyes. Father, I thank You that my eyes are filled and covered with the blood of Jesus Christ. Father, I thank You that no familiar spirit or demon from Hell will use my body as a way of monitoring for witches, warlocks, demons, the devil, Satan, and Hell. We break the covenant with familiar spirits now, in Jesus Christ's name. Father, I thank You that my bloodline is free of anything that desires to look, operate, and function in the wrong realm. I thank You, Lord, that my eyes belong to you and no one else.

Father, we break the covenant with any form of lust that enters through the eye to cause pain or adultery. Father, thank You that my ears belong to You in the name of Jesus Christ. I thank You that Your blood covers me from the crown of my head to the sole of my feet, in the name of Jesus Christ. I thank You that I see through Your eyes in the name of Jesus Christ. Father, I break the covenant with everything on my bloodline that will cause me to see from the wrong realm in the name of Jesus Christ. Father, I thank You that your blood purifies my bloodline. Hallelujah in the name of Jesus Christ.

Father, I thank You in the name of Jesus Christ that I will have good discernment and discern who is true and who is false. Father, I thank You that I will see with Your heart in the name of Jesus Christ, and I will not be pulled on by my heartstrings in the name of Jesus Christ. Father, sharpen my discernment. Father, let me see You as you see me in the name of Jesus Christ. Holy Spirit, show me myself, and Holy Spirit, show me Thyself in the name of Jesus Christ. Father, thank You that You will send good Christian friends and that I will see their hearts prior to them coming into my circumference in the name of Jesus Christ. Father, I thank You that I will not be deceived by a dark veil over my eyes in the name of Jesus Christ. Father, I thank You, hallelujah, for Your love for me and that You did not allow me to be fooled by the hands of the enemy in the name of Jesus Christ.

Father, thank You for removing all anger, frustration, pain, resentment, bitterness, and anything else. Father, remove anything that is a part of my emotional, physical, and mental DNA that will alter how I see people in the name of Jesus Christ. Father, thank You that I will see people through Your eyes, not mine, in the name of Jesus.

Father, I thank You in the name of Jesus Christ that I will stand boldly and declare Your glory on earth as I see what You are doing in the lives of my brother and sister in Christ. I thank You that I will not stand in judgment or solidarity against my brother or sister in Christ. Father, I thank you that I would stand and see them as your true soldiers, your dear children, that you have called for such a time as this.

Father, I thank You that I will not stand in jealousy and resentment against my brother and sister in Christ, in the name of Jesus. Father, I thank You that I will not judge people wrongfully because of my own inner issues, in the name of Jesus Christ. Father, thank You that I will always look in the mirror at myself first, knowing that the blood of Jesus Christ works for all who believe in the name of Jesus Christ. Father, thank You that I have your heart and that I will see the world as you see it in the name of Jesus Christ.

Father, thank You for Your blood that covers my optical lobe; keeps it pure, holy, and righteous before You in the name of Jesus Christ. Oh God, do not allow the enemy to confuse my mind through my eyes, in the name of Jesus Christ. Jesus, help me to read Your Word and to see it as truth and not just a good storybook in the name of Jesus Christ. Help me to see Your Word through Your heart, in the name of Jesus Christ. Father, thank You that when You bring people into the house of the Lord who desire change, healing, and restoration, we will see them through Your eyes and Your heart and that we will not judge them and make them feel condemned. Father, Your Word declares in Romans 8:1 (KJV) that there is therefore now no condemnation to them that are in Christ Jesus who walk not after the flesh but after the spirit.

Father, I thank You that we will have mercy on those who need mercy and that we will guide and be patient with the process You're working on with our brothers and sisters in Christ, no matter what we see them walking through. Father, thank You that we will see things as You see them. Father, thank You that we will not look at fiery trials that come to test our faith as something terrible, but we will look at this as another dimension and another weight of oil that You are pouring out on us in the name of Jesus Christ.

Thank You for letting us see Your Word as a revelation for today. Give us understanding and help us to understand the mysteries of it in the name of Jesus Christ.

❧

<u>Cerebellum</u>

Father, thank You for the cerebellum part of our brains. I thank You, Father, that we have the ability to reason and to think clearly in the name of Jesus Christ. Father, Your Word declares in Psalms 127:1 (KJV) that except the LORD builds a house, the laborers will be building in vain. I thank You, Father, that You have made us master builders for Your glory. I thank You that we hear Your voice through our cerebellum with clear, concise instructions on how to build Your house in the name of Jesus. Father, just as You gave Noah instructions for the ark, give us instructions on how to love our communities through servant-hood. Teach us how to build and love the body of Christ with genuine hearts and pure servitude unto the Lord in the name of Jesus Christ. Father, show us how to build up families, encourage ourselves and others with the love of Jesus Christ.

Father, take us behind the veil! Give us instructions for our countries. Give us instructions for our cities, for school systems, and for the government. Show us how to build them up in prayer, the Word, and deeds in the name of Jesus Christ. Sharpen our discernment. Show us what we should touch and what we shouldn't touch in the name of Jesus Christ. Show us, dear Lord, how to bring Your glory to a dying land and world. We desire to do it Your way, or no way at all, in the name of Jesus Christ.

Father, make us master builders of light and skillful demolition teams of darkness in the name of Jesus Christ. Father, Your Word declares in Psalms 133:1 (KJV): "Oh, how good and pleasant it is for brethren to dwell together in unity." God, build the house of God through us. We yield the fruit of our minds, hearts, spirits, souls, wealth, and health to You.

We appreciate Your sacrifice of dying for us on the cross, so now, Father, we do the same for You in the name of Jesus Christ. Master builder, chief cornerstone, build through us in the name of Jesus Christ. Help us to uplift our brothers and sisters in prayer in the name of Jesus Christ. We stand with them and will not be the enemies of the Kingdom of God. We declare and decree that we are blessings to Your house and Kingdom, not curses. We will sow in time, talent, and treasure dearest Jesus, in the name of Jesus Christ. Father, we thank You that it is so in Jesus's name, Amen!

Father, I thank You for the limbs of our bodies. I thank You that we will dance before You as David did in the Bible, according to 2 Samuel 6:14–22. Father David danced with all of his might. He appreciated what You had done for the children of Israel and how You delivered them from the hands of the enemy. Father, I thank You for the radical praise pouring out of us in the name of Jesus Christ. I thank You that we will give You what's due without worrying about what others have to say about us.

Father, we break the covenant with the spirit of pride and make a covenant with gratefulness. Father, we are grateful for all You have done for us in the name of Jesus Christ. Spirit of pride, Leviathan, you are a liar. May the falsehood of your demonic smoke, your demonic miracles, and your demonic words all be roasted by the true fire of God now in the name of Jesus Christ. Our gratitude to the Father outweighs your demonic powers. Our gratitude to God will push us to praise and worship God like never before. We will not be ashamed to worship the Father in His tabernacle or wherever we may be Lord, we thank You that we remember what Your Word declares in Psalm 107:1, "For he is good, and his mercy endures for all generations." Lord, we have decided to live a life of prayer, praise, and servitude to You in the name of Jesus Christ, and we will not allow anyone to deter us! It is so, in Jesus's name, Amen!

10

BODY OF CHRIST

Father, I thank You for the body of Christ. I thank You that Your Word declares in Psalms 133:1, "Oh how good and pleasant it is for brethren to dwell together in unity." Father, I thank You that we are unified as the body of Christ. I thank You, Lord, that we will stand together as one voice, one frequency, and with one worship unto You. I thank You, Father, that we, as the body of Christ, will all come together to worship You as ruler and King. Father, I thank You that we will not fall into agreement with anything that isn't aligned with Your holy Word. I thank You, Lord, that together we will stand and pray for this world and for our country. Father, I thank You that we will stand together as one in the body of Christ, lifting our brothers and sisters in Word and deed. I thank You that we will not destroy our brothers and sisters in Christ with judgmental words, curses, lies, gossip, malice, envy, jealousy, and hurt. Lord, I thank You that we will unify against the enemy and recognize that Satan is the real adversary, not each other, in the name of Jesus Christ.

Father, I thank You for taming the tongue of every believer in Christ Jesus. I thank You, Lord, that we will only say what You want us to say and do what You tell us to do. We drive the demon of gossip and lies away from us in the name of Jesus Christ. Be roasted by fire now! The legal blood of Jesus Christ is against you! Father, I thank You that we will always be led by Your Spirit and not another, in the name of Jesus Christ. Dear Jesus, Your Word declares in John 10:27, "My sheep hear my voice, and I know them, and they follow me." Lord, I thank You that we hear Your voice clearly and that we will not follow another voice. Lord, clear our ears of all clutters so that we can clearly hear Your voice in the name of Jesus Christ. Lord, I thank You that we are supporters of the gospel within the body of Christ.

I thank You for bringing the people of God together to stand in unity against the enemy. Lord, I thank You that we will connect more with our fellow co-laborers in the gospel in the name of Jesus Christ. Connect us to our God-given tribe. Connect us to other warriors, such as us, in the name of Jesus Christ. Remove every counterfeit. Lord, Your Word declares in John 4:1, "Beloved, do not believe every spirit, but test the spirits to see whether they are from God because many false prophets have gone out into the world." I thank You for sharpening our discernment for us to see, know, and maneuver in You in the name of Jesus Christ.

Lord, I thank You we will serve You with gladness and not with competition. Lord, I thank You that we will remember that You have made us all unique and wonderful, according to Psalms 139:13–14. We stand together; we war together as the body of Christ; therefore, we will all win together in the name of Jesus Christ. Lord, You are in control of our lives, and we will carry Your Word out in obedience. We walk by faith, Father, not by sight, according to 2 Corinthians 5:7 (KJV). We walk in obedience not because of what we can see but because we trust You with our very lives. We don't have to see it Jesus, to know that

You are going to do it. Do it for us, God, in the name of Jesus Christ. Father,

I thank You that the body of Christ is standing together, unified unto You as one. Father, we declare and decree that Galatians 5:1 is our portion. We cry out to You, Father, the author and finisher of our faith. We cry out to You for healing and deliverance for the body. We cry out to You for peace within the body of Christ. We cry to You, oh God, for pure and undefiled love within the body of Christ. Your Word declares in 1 Corinthians 13:7 that love conquers all. We declare that the body of Christ is free of physical, mental, and emotional distress and disease because of Your blood and love. Lord, Your Word declares that we are healed by the wound in your side, according to Isaiah 53:5. Father, together as the body of Christ, we stand and agree with Your legal sacrificial blood that you shed for us in the name of Jesus Christ. Father, I thank You that Your blood is renewing our love for You right now in the name of Jesus Christ. I thank You, Lord, that Your blood will be preached, taught, and counted as sacred again in the body of Christ. Lord, I thank You that we will not deviate from our purpose in the body of Christ, which is to preach Your death, burial, and resurrection to a dying world.

Father, I thank You that we, as believers in the body of Christ, will come together to win the lost for Your glory. Give us the passion to win souls again in the name of Jesus Christ. I thank You, Lord, that You are destroying a false sense of entitlement within the body of Christ. I thank You that we will put down our titles and take the mandate and the mantle to win souls for You again, Lord, in the name of Jesus Christ. Fill Your house, God, with those who are spiritually sick. Let the church be the hospital for broken souls again, Lord, in the name of Jesus Christ. Lord, send us, and we will go! Hallelujah! Lord, I thank You that You are moving right now.

I thank You that the spirit of evangelism will return to the body of Christ right now in the name of Jesus Christ again. You told us in 2 Timothy 2:4-5, "But watch thou in all things, endure afflictions, do the work of an evangelist, make full proof of thy ministry." Lord, please do not allow us to forget what You have done for us and where You brought us from. Lest we forget God, keep us gracefully broken before You. Keep us at Your feet in the name of Jesus Christ. Father, I thank You that we will not talk about, judge, or ridicule the lost but give them to you. We will show them Your love, grace, and mercy toward Your people. Father, I thank You that we will remember when we received Jesus as Lord and Savior over our lives and allow Your compassion and passion for souls to be rekindled within us. Help us, Lord. Help us, dear Jesus. Send a fresh wind of Your Spirit over the body of Christ. Send revival!

Your Word tells us in Acts 3:19, "Repent, then, and turn to God, so that your sins may be wiped out, that times of refreshing may come from the Lord." Turning to God brings times of refreshing. Revive prayer and intercession in churches. Revive the love for ministry and You, God, back to the body of Christ in the name of Jesus Christ. Please, dear Jesus, do not allow us to forget where we come from and what You brought us out of. Help us to remain humble and at Your feet. Help us to remember that the blood of Jesus Christ will wash anyone who calls upon Your name. Help us, oh God, to be faithful to the cross. Help us to continue to hold up the blood-stained banner of Jesus Christ. Help us, Jesus! In the name of Jesus Christ! Let there be a refreshing of Your spirit upon the body of Christ like never before. Give us God encounters, dear Lord, in the name of Jesus Christ!

Meet us in our prayer closets. Meet us in our cars; meet us in our small groups. Meet us in our homes. Meet us at our jobs. Meet us everywhere, and anywhere we go, dear Jesus. We give You permission to invade our lives. We want Your glory, dear Jesus. Hallelujah! Sanctify our minds. Destroy our will. Jesus, we thank You for the fresh fire that will hit the body of Christ in the name of Jesus Christ. We thank You for revealing who You are and what You've done for us. Dearest Jesus, help us in the body of Christ to remember that without You, there is no us. Lord, we thank You for all You are doing for us even now.

We declare that the body of Christ is healed, whole, and set free. In the name of Jesus Christ. Amen.

<u>Spirit of Cain - Murder</u>

Father, in the name of Jesus Christ, by fire, we demolish the spirit of Cain within the body of Christ. Father, I thank You that we take what you have given to us seriously. I thank You that we will not be as Cain in Genesis 4, as one that works within the marketplace and does not give You our best. Father, I thank You that we will dig into Your Word and that we will see what is required of us. Father, Your Word declares in Malachi 3:10 (KJV), "Bring ye all the tithes into the storehouse, that there may be meat in mine house, and prove me now herewith, saith the Lord of hosts, if I will not open you the windows of Heaven, and pour you out a blessing, that there shall not be room enough to receive it." Father, I thank You that we are not stingy. I thank You that we are givers who are led by Your Spirit. Father, I thank You in the name of Jesus Christ that we would not focus on where the tithes and offerings are going but on the assignment of bringing all tithes and offerings into the storehouse. Dearest Jesus, I thank You that we will not only sow monetarily but also in time and talent. Father, we present our lives to You as a living sacrifice, holy and acceptable, for it is our reasonable service in the name of Jesus Christ, according to Romans 8:12 (KJV). Father, I thank You that we will not be jealous of our brothers and sisters in Christ and that we will celebrate what You are doing in and through the lives of other believers in the name of

Jesus Christ. We drive out by fire, gossip, curses, lies, and deceit that may try to surface amongst the people of God, dearest Jesus. We will not murder the body of Christ with our tongues, dear Lord, in the name of Jesus Christ. We will not murder anything that may be walking through a terrible time, even if they are being blessed. We will continue to lift our brothers and sisters in prayer in the name of Jesus Christ. We declare and decree life over the body of Christ. May the spirit of Cain (murder) be destroyed by fire in the name of Jesus Christ. May the spirit of Cain (murder) be murdered by the legal blood of Jesus Christ. Father, I thank You that it's done in Jesus Christ's name, amen!

Spirit of Korah - Rebellion

Father, we come against the spirit of Korah (rebellion) in the body of Christ. Lord, Your Word declares in 1 Samuel 15:23 (KJV), "For rebellion is as the sin of witchcraft, and stubbornness is as iniquity and idolatry. Because thou hast rejected the Word of the Lord, he hath also rejected thee from being king." Father, I thank You that, as the body of Christ, we will not rebel against the truth of Your Word. I thank You that we will walk in integrity and not look for loopholes around, walking in the truth and not rebellion in the name of Jesus Christ. Jesus, we break the neck of rebellion by obeying Your voice and truths in the Word of God, in the name of Jesus Christ. We choose life. We choose freedom and holiness in the name of Jesus Christ. Father, I thank You that our rightful inheritance from you as heirs with God and joint heirs with Jesus Christ will not be forfeited due to rebellion, fear, anxiety, and lust in the name of Jesus Christ. Father, I thank You that we will willingly obey Your Word and Your voice that proceeds out of the mouth of Your woman or manservants.

Father, I thank You that we will not gather anyone together as Korah did in Numbers the 16th chapter to fight against the instructions of the Lord in the name of Jesus Christ. We dismantle every evil heresy, Father, that may arise in local churches, homes, and in our communities within the body of Christ. Jesus, we thank You for breaking every fault and finding the spirit of the people of God in the name of Jesus Christ. I declare and decree that we will look for Jesus when we walk into the room. I thank You, Lord, that You will sharpen our discernment and destroy our opinions. Opinions do not matter, Father, in Your presence, in the name of Jesus Christ. Father,

I thank You that we will receive, apply, and act upon the Word of God that has been spoken into our lives through the servants of God. God, I thank You that leaders will not respond to the Korah's in their lives as Moses did in Numbers 16th chapter but as pure vessels unto You. Lord, we thank You for healing every leader and every armor bearer who has been affected by the demonic influence that has proceeded out of the mouth of broken leaders within the body of Christ in the name of Jesus Christ. Father, we drive out gossip and false perceptions in the name of Jesus Christ.

Father, we thank You that it's done. We thank you that we will not judge or wrongfully talk about what God-ordained leaders are doing within the body of Christ. We will stand together as one in the name of Jesus Christ, amen.

Spirit of Balaam—Spirit of Error and Greed

Father, I thank You for freedom from the spirit of Balaam within the body of Christ. Lord, Your Word declares in 1 Timothy 6:10 (KJV), "For the love of money is the root of all evil: which while some coveted after, they have erred from the faith, and pierced themselves through with many sorrows." Father, I thank You that we love Your Word more than money. Father, I thank You that we will remain integral with the money You allow to come to and through our hands. I thank You that we are faithful, according to Malachi 3:10, "Bring ye all the tithes into the storehouse, that there may be meat in mine house, and prove me now herewith, saith the Lord of hosts, if I will not open you the windows of Heaven, and pour you out a blessing, that there shall not be room enough to receive it."

Father, I thank You that we will bring what is Yours to the house of God by faith and trust You with the 90% You allow us to have in the name of Jesus Christ. Father, we destroy by Your holy fire, the spirit of greed and cast it away from the body of Christ. We thank You, Lord, that we will not covet anything from anyone, whether monetarily, skillfully, or even mentally, in the name of Jesus Christ. Father, I thank You that we, the body of Christ, will not be as Balaam and cause discord and confusion in the body of Christ because of jealousy, envy, and greed. Father, bring us together as one in Jesus Christ's name.

<u>Spirit of Jezebel—Spirit of Control, Manipulation, and Intimidation</u>

God, we push Jezebel out of the window in the name of Jesus Christ. May she fall off her high horse break her neck and be embarrassed in the name of Jesus Christ. We thank You, Father, that the spirit of control and manipulation is broken off the people of God that has been induced by Jezebel in the name of Jesus Christ. I bind the retaliation and backlash that Jezebel sends due to her not having her way in the name of Jesus Christ. We rid the body of Christ, the church, schools, jobs, ministries, homes, legislative seats, corporate seats, and any hierarchy not listed here, of her power in the name of Jesus Christ.

We declare and decree that the third eye that she utilizes is burned by fire in the name of Jesus Christ. We come against the divination she releases through wrongful prayers and false fire in the name of Jesus Christ. We declare and decree that Jezabel will not be able to divide the nation of our homes, minds, spirits, or souls in the name of Jesus Christ. We take the sword of the Spirit and slay all of her flunkies. Every demon that works for her, be destroyed by the Word of God, now in the name of Jesus Christ.

The Word of God declares in Hebrews 4:12, "For the Word of God is quick, and powerful, and sharper than any two-edged sword, piercing even to the dividing asunder of soul and spirit, and of the joints and marrow, and is a discerner of the thoughts and intents of the heart." Word of God, annihilate this dark principality in the name of Jesus Christ. Jezebel, your time is up. You are defeated. Leave the body of Christ. Leave and never return. Pack your bags and go! In the name of Jesus Christ. You do not scare us, and we are NOT intimidated by you! You have no power. None! In the name of Jesus Christ. All demonic spirits that you have employed, we take rank over you in the spirit and fire them in the name of Jesus Christ. We thank You, dear Lord, that it's done in the name of Jesus Christ, amen!

11

PHYSICAL BODY

As believers in Christ Jesus, it is imperative that we take care of our physical bodies. Oftentimes, we watch our fellow brothers and sisters in Christ die prematurely due to not being good stewards of their temples. In order for us as people of God to carry the true weight of Glory from the Father, we must eat healthy, exercise, drink plenty of water, and refrain from stress. This is something that the Father has had to teach me. Just because you can buy Dunkin Donuts doesn't mean that you should. Just because you can afford to go out to eat every day doesn't mean that you should. Oftentimes prior to going on my weight loss journey, it would take me almost 2 weeks to recover in my physical body after preaching, teaching, working the altar, and casting out demons. Do You know why? It was because I was 150 pounds overweight. I was an emotional eater and instead of dealing with my internal pain, rejection, and hurt, food was one of my drugs of choice. The weight of God would sit on me, and God would use me mightily but because of the natural weight, I would feel like I had been hit by a freight train afterward. This was a huge door for major retaliation for me. Many times, when I was overweight, I would receive a lot of backlashes from the demonic spirits that I just cast out! The demons knew that once the spirit of the Lord had died down a little bit, that they could come and attach or even try to enter me. This was all because I didn't have any discipline. I had to repent and lose the natural weight to receive the fullness of my mantel. What I was going through wasn't the devil. It was me. I had to fight through all kinds of medication, doctor visits, and injections just to stay alive. I thank God that I am totally healed because of my choosing to be disciplined in taking care of my health holistically! Today I pray that you have a change of heart and decide if you aren't already to take care of your natural temples. This is most definitely pleasing to the Father. Let's pray about our physical bodies now in Jesus Christ's name.

Father, I thank You that Your Word declares that my body is the temple of the Holy Ghost in 1 Corinthians 6:19. I thank You for creating me and making me unique and beautiful. I thank You for leaving us the comforter of the Holy Spirit to dwell within our temples. Lord, make us good stewards over our bodies in the name of Jesus Christ. I thank You that we will take care of our bodies with proper sleep, nourishment, doctoral care, a proper diet, and exercise. I thank You, Lord, that every part of our bodies functions and operates as You created them to be in the name of Jesus Christ, amen.

The Head

Father, thank You for our heads. Your Word declares in Isaiah 1:5, "Why should ye be stricken anymore? Ye will revolt more and more: the whole head is sick, and the whole heart faint." Father, we are healed in our heads! I declare it to be so in the name of Jesus Christ. Father, I thank You that our heads are filled with wisdom, knowledge, and amazing creativity in the name of Jesus Christ. Father, I thank You that our brains are full of witty inventions and ideas, in the name of Jesus Christ. I thank You that we are thought leaders. I thank You that wisdom will speak loudly out of our mouths and from our brains in the name of Jesus Christ.

Father, we release Your legal blood to cover the gates of our minds from amnesia, memory loss, and brain fogginess in the name of Jesus Christ. We thank You, Lord, that we are free of random headaches and tightness around our heads in the name of Jesus Christ. We thank You that brain tumors, cancer of the brain, sickness of the mind, corruption of the mind, and schizophrenia of any kind will never be our portion in the name of Jesus Christ. We thank You, Father, that every blood vessel, every muscle, and every nerve ending is functional as You created them to be from the foundation of the earth in the name of Jesus Christ. Father, we thank You that brain strokes, aneurysms, head colds, and bacteria that would affect any part of our head and brain will never be our portion in the name of Jesus Christ. We break the covenant with any sickness of the head and brain that may still be lingering or connected to us through bloodline covenants in the name of Jesus Christ. We thank You that we are fully healed in the name of Jesus Christ, amen!

Our Hands

J esus, I thank You for our hands. I thank You, Lord, that our hands will bring great wealth to us. We thank You, dearest Jesus, that wealth and riches are within our houses, according to Psalms 112:3. Father, we thank You in the name of Jesus Christ that our hands will bring comfort to those who are in need of comfort, create new things, war in prayer, and bring healing to all that we come in contact with in the name of Jesus

Christ. Lord, You have called my fingers to fight and my hands to war, according to Psalms 144:1. We will war in the spirit with our hands for our creativity, for our families, for the comfort and peace of others, and most of all, for the body of Christ. Father, we war and win in the name of Jesus Christ. Father, I thank You that every nerve ending and blood vessel within our hands is functional and without failure. I thank You, Lord, that everything our hands touch will turn to prophetic gold. Father, we chase away arthritis, carpal tunnel syndrome, and callused skin-holding bacteria on our hands in the name of Jesus Christ.

Father, we declare and decree that every part of our hands will forever work as You created them from the foundations of the earth in the name of Jesus Christ.

∼

The Mouth

Father, I thank You that the words of our mouth and the meditation of our hearts are acceptable in thy sight in the name of Jesus Christ, according to Psalms 19:14. I declare and decree that we, the body of Christ, will speak life with our mouths and not destruction. I thank You, Lord, that we will use our tongues and mouths to give You praise, glory, and honor. Father, I thank You that we will use our mouths and voices to sing songs to You and for intercession. I thank You, Father, that we will utilize our mouths to release love letters in the spirit back to You in the name of Jesus Christ.

Father, we drive away all foul sickness and disease that the enemy would try to send to Your people in the name of Jesus Christ. We drive away diseases associated with gingivitis, rotten teeth, tonsil stones, bad tonsils, bad adenoids, and thick tongues in the name of Jesus Christ. We ask that You forgive us for not taking care of our hygiene as we should have when we could have dearest Jesus. We drive out the spirit of infirmity in the name of Jesus Christ.

We break the covenant with infection, toothache, and any issue of pain that may hit our mouths in the name of Jesus Christ. Jesus, we know that You are the ultimate healer, so we ask You to intervene and be our portion in the name of Jesus Christ. Jesus, You are Lord over our mouths! With our mouths, we will declare Your Word and peace on earth in the name of Jesus Christ. Use us, dear God! I thank You, Father, for healing those who have cleft lips, lisp tongues, and those who stutter when they speak in the name of Jesus Christ.

Father, we drive out the spirit of fear that causes stuttering in the name of Jesus Christ. I thank You, Father, that every speech impediment is broken by the legal blood of Jesus Christ. Father, those who fear speaking before crowds and speaking to people in intimate circles, I thank You for giving them a new boldness to speak Your Word with truth, clarity, and fire in the name of Jesus Christ. Father, allow the minor defects in their natural bodies to be a great testimony of Your power. Heal them and use them, oh God, all for Your glory in the name of Jesus Christ.

I thank You, Father, for healthy teeth. I thank You that our teeth are great grinders and that we can properly chew our food for digestion. We bind and rebuke deficiencies in the amount of calcium within our bodies in the name of Jesus Christ. We thank You, Father, that we will take care of our teeth and that we will not give in to eating a lot of sugar, ice, and other things that would destroy them in the name of Jesus Christ. Father, You are worthy! We thank You that it is done in the name of Jesus Christ, amen!

Our Stomachs

Father, we thank You for giving us a house to keep the food we consume— our stomachs. We thank You for how You made the human body! God, You are amazing, and we stand in awe of Your marvelous work. Man is your masterpiece! God, we thank You that our stomachs are the right size and not overly stretched because of overeating and lust. We drive gluttony away from us, God, in the name of Jesus Christ. Your Word declares in 1 Corinthians 3:17 (KJV) that "if anyone destroys God's temple, God will destroy that person; for God's temple is sacred, and you together are that temple." God, we repent for not taking good care of our bellies by not eating the right things and being out of sync with Your voice about our diet in the name of Jesus Christ. Father, show us how to eat according to our blood types. Show us how to cook healthy in the name of Jesus Christ. Lord, protect the lining of our stomachs. Keep it in alignment, and do not allow it to be overly acidic in the name of Jesus Christ.

We drive acid reflux, a sour stomach, indigestion, heartburn, and anything of the like away from us in the name of Jesus Christ. Father, I thank You that our stomachs are normal and how You created them from the foundation of the earth in the name of Jesus Christ. We break the covenant with anything that may be on our bloodlines in conjunction with our stomachs in the name of Jesus Christ. We drive out by the fire of God cancer, tumors, the inability to digest food, swelling of the belly, and anything else that we may not be aware of, Father, in the name of Jesus Christ.

We drive out by fire every demonic snake or demonic snake egg that Satan has sent to us in the form of a python to coil up and bind up our dreams and destinies in the name of Jesus Christ. We also drive out demonic snails from the marine kingdom that works in conjunction with the underworld to slither and hide in moist, molded places in our lives, Lord, in the name of Jesus Christ.

Father, help us to overturn everything in our lives that would be an open door for the enemy to enter our lives in the name of Jesus Christ. Jesus, heal us from everything within our stomachs, known and unknown, in the name of Jesus Christ. I thank You that it is done in Jesus's name, amen!

<u>Feet</u>

Father, I thank You that Your Word declares that You have made my feet as hind feet, according to Psalms 18:33. Father, we thank You that our feet are functional and that we can praise You with dance in the name of Jesus Christ. Father, I thank You that we can run through troops and leap over walls. We thank You that every one of our toes is in existence and is functional in the name of Jesus Christ. Lord, thank You for calling our feet blessed because we publish the gospel. We bind, rebuke, and refuse any irregularity with our feet in the name of Jesus Christ.

I thank You that all nerve endings work and will not be affected by any disease in our bodies, in the name of Jesus Christ. Father, I thank You that we have great circulation in our feet, beautiful and healthy toenails, and great tread under our feet in the name of Jesus Christ. I thank You that we will continue to take care of the hygiene of our feet consistently in the name of Jesus Christ.

Father, I thank You that we are trailblazers in the name of Jesus Christ. I thank You that as we war in intercession and prayer, fire is released over our homes, jobs, and ministries in the name of Jesus Christ. As we stomp our feet over territories and regions, God, we declare, and decree new territory claimed for you in the name of Jesus Christ. We thank You, Father, that as we walk forward in Your things, we will leave a trail of Your fire wherever we go in the name of Jesus Christ. Territories, we take you back for the kingdom of God in the name of Jesus Christ. Land, rivers, and streams, we claim you now for the Father in the name of Jesus Christ.

The Word of God tells us in Joshua 1:9 (KJV), "Have not I commanded thee? Be strong and of good courage; be not afraid, neither be thou dismayed: for the Lord thy God is with thee whithersoever thou goest." Father, I thank You for ordering every footstep we take. We are forever led by Your spirit. We will go where You tell us to go, dearest Jesus, in the name of Jesus Christ. We will go in faith without fear, knowing that You are with us in the name of Jesus Christ.

Father, we thank You for causing the lame to walk and the crippled and paraplegic to run in the name of Jesus Christ. We thank You, Jesus, for being the healer of club feet, ingrown toenails, and fungus of the foot in the name of Jesus Christ. Club Feet! Straighten out in Jesus Christ's name. Crippled legs, para-plegic bodies, be healed in the name of Jesus Christ! Now! Lame, rise, and walk now in the name of Jesus Christ! The Bible states that by the stripes of Jesus Christ, we are already healed, which makes you illegal. You are trespassing in our bodies in the name of Jesus Christ. God be glorified and remove each of the listed demonic spirits in the name of Jesus Christ. It is so, in Jesus Christ's name, amen!

Father, we thank You that we have the ability to walk in freedom and wholeness in the name of Jesus Christ. Father, let Your will be done through our feet. We totally surrender them to You for Your use. I thank You that it's done in the name of Jesus Christ, amen!

<h1 style="text-align:center"><u>Eyes</u></h1>

Father, I thank You for giving us two eyes to see in the name of Jesus Christ. Your Word declares in Matthew 6:22–23: "The eye is the lamp of the body. If your eyes are healthy, your whole body will be full of light. But if your eyes are unhealthy, your whole body will be full of darkness." Thank You for making our eyes spiritually and naturally healthy in the name of Jesus Christ. Thank You for chasing darkness away from our eyes in the name of Jesus Christ. We thank You that the windows of our souls are not clouded with divination, clairvoyance, the spirit of Ra, 3rd eyes (the all-seeing eye), crystal balls, and demonic-looking glasses in the name of Jesus Christ. I thank You, Father, that we only see through your Holy Spirit, as you allow.

Father, I thank You for removing every dark veil from our eyes so that we can have pure perception and knowledge of situations, things around us, and the people around us in the name of Jesus Christ. We command every dark veil to be roasted by fire now in the name of Jesus Christ. I thank You, Lord, that we see as You see and no other way. Thank You for your legal blood that covers our eyes in the name of Jesus Christ. Father, be glorified! Hallelujah!

Father, I thank You for being the healer of our eyes. We break covenant with color blindness, legal blindness, distorted vision, cataracts, and glaucoma. We command them to dry up in the name of Jesus Christ. We declare and decree that we see clearly through our natural eyes in the name of Jesus Christ. We see color without any malfunction or distortion in the name of Jesus Christ, amen! Father, we declare and decree that tumors are dissipating from the eye gates in the name of Jesus Christ. Every tumor catch fire now. Be burned with the fire of the Holy Ghost. You are illegal! You do not belong in our bodies. Be gone now, in the name of Jesus Christ. We war against you with the legal blood of Jesus Christ, amen!

Lord, I thank You for our pupils. I thank You that our eyes are able to adjust to light as needed. Father, I thank You for the ciliary bodies of our eyes. I thank You that every structural muscle within our eyes works as you created them to work, Father, in the name of Jesus Christ. I thank You that our eyes can focus and determine what they are looking at in conjunction with the brain, in the name of Jesus Christ.

Father, I thank You that our corneas are able to transmit, sharpen, and clarify light to our eyes in the name of Jesus Christ. I thank you that the irises of our eyes are the right color and not distorted by sickness of any kind hidden within the human body, in the name of Jesus Christ. Father, I thank You that our irises work properly and adjust naturally to light as needed. I thank You that they will not allow too much or too little light to enter our eyes in the name of Jesus Christ. I thank You, Jesus, that our retinas are healthy and not easily torn in the name of Jesus Christ.

And lastly, God, I thank You that our complete optical nervous systems bundle up millions of nerve endings with precision in the name of Jesus Christ. I thank You that they will forever partner with our brains to fire the right images to the mind and eyegate in the name of Jesus Christ. Father, our eyes are completely healthy, healed, and whole in the name of Jesus Christ. Jesus, You are Lord over our eyes, and we give our eyes to You again in the name of Jesus Christ. Keep lust away from our eyes. Keep greed away from our eyes, according to Matthew 5:28–29. We chase adultery away from our eyes in the name of Jesus Christ. Perversion of any kind, we shine the light of Jesus Christ on you! Be removed from our lives now, in the name of Jesus Christ. Lord, I thank You that our eyes will not wander away from You and our spouses. I thank You for keeping us, oh

God, in the name of Jesus Christ. Dearest Lord, our eyes belong to You and You alone in the name of Jesus Christ. Amen!

<u>Ears</u>

Father, I thank You that Your Word declares in Matthew 11:15, "He that has an ear let him hear." Father, I thank You that we have ears to hear Your voice and not a stranger's voice in the name of Jesus Christ. I thank You that Your voice resounds in our ears in prayer, worship, study, travel, and everyday life. Father, I thank You that we hear Your voice through our ears and that it guides us daily. Father, Your Word declares in John 10:27–28 (KJV), "My sheep hear my voice, and I know them, and they follow me: And I give unto them eternal life; and they shall never perish, neither shall any man pluck them out of my hand." I thank You for covering our spiritual and natural ears from falsehoods, gossip, lies, drama, infidelity, corruption, wrong music, wrong preaching, maliciousness, and pain in the name of Jesus Christ. Father, because we value the oil of God in our lives, we break the covenant with anything or anyone that will try to fill our ears with drama and release flies on our oil. God, our ears belong to You, and we trust You with them all the days of our lives in the name of Jesus Christ, amen!

Father, I thank You for our outer ears in the name of Jesus Christ. Father, I thank You that the auricles and auditory parts of our ears work exceptionally well in the name of Jesus Christ. I thank You that we can hear sound, music, laughter, and even ourselves in the name of Jesus Christ. Father, I thank You that our external ears are protected from all bacteria, disease, infection, and damage. Cover our eardrums in the name of Jesus Christ. I thank You, Father, that we will not play loud sound decibels that will destroy or damage our eardrums in the name of Jesus Christ.

Father, I thank You for destroying every attack on eardrums by fire in the name of Jesus Christ. We drive out muteness, deaf and dumb spirits, and severe sinus problems (airway spirits) that cause infection to drain on the ears in the name of Jesus Christ. You deaf and dumb spirit, we anker you to the bottom of Sheol's floor in the name of Jesus Christ. We destroy your dark powers by the legal blood of Jesus Christ, and we say that we are free in the name of Jesus Christ. Our ears are free, and it is so in the name of Jesus Christ, amen!

Father, please keep our eustachian tubes free of sinus drainage and bacterial debris in the name of Jesus Christ. We command all sinus pressure that affects how we hear out of our eustachian tubes to be removed from us in the name of Jesus Christ. The translation of how we hear frequency, sound waves, and even our own voices will not be touched or destroyed in the name of Jesus Christ. Do it for Your glory, oh God, in the name of Jesus Christ.

We declare even now, God, that hearing aids will become obsolete! Hearing aids, be burned by fire now in the name of Jesus Christ. Ears, pop open! Hear! Function! In the name of Jesus Christ! God, I thank You that You will give children, young and old, men and women, the opportunity to hear again in the name of Jesus Christ. Your name, frequency, and sound be glorified in the ear, oh God, in the name of Jesus Christ, amen!

Father, I thank You for covering the ossicles of our ears in the name of Jesus Christ. I thank You that the malleus, incus, and stapes of our ears remain intact, unharmed, and healthy all the days of our lives in the name of Jesus Christ. Father, we thank You for healing and sustaining our inner ears in the name of Jesus Christ.

Father, I thank You that the cochlea, vestibule, and semicircular canals all work together for hearing and balance. I thank

You that every nerve ending is completely whole in the name of Jesus Christ. Father, we thank You that our equilibrium is accurate, that our receptors receive, and that every one of our nerve endings works, in the name of Jesus Christ. Our bodies are balanced and stable. We have no problem standing due to our equilibrium being off balance in the name of Jesus Christ. Father, it is done! We give You glory for it in Jesus Christ's name, amen!

$$\sim$$

Internal organs

Father, I thank You for every internal organ You have given us. Jesus, help us to be good stewards over our bodies in the name of Jesus Christ. We thank You for our livers, dear Lord. We thank You that they're healthy—strong bile filters that carry nutrients in our bodies to where they should be in the name of Jesus Christ. Father, I thank You for our natural hearts. I thank You that they are free of arrhythmia, heart disease, broken valve sickness, and anything else that shouldn't be there in the name of Jesus Christ. I thank You, Father, that we will guard our hearts in prayer and diet. We thank You for strong heart valves and good blood flow throughout our hearts in the name of Jesus Christ. I thank You, Father, that we will only allow You to consume our hearts and that we will be in sync with Your heartbeat, for You are our heartbeat, and we love You!

Father, I thank You that our kidneys are healthy. I thank You that they purify our blood and properly rid waste from our bodies in the name of Jesus Christ. I thank You, Lord, that our kidneys will continue to funnel the nutrients we obtain from the foods we consume to the proper places in our bodies in the name of Jesus Christ. Lord, I thank You that we will choose good, healthy food, not consume strong drinks, and be aware of our surroundings that may have contaminants in the air, in the name of Jesus

Christ. Father, we bind and rebuke any kind of kidney failure in the name of Jesus Christ.

We take authority over the spirit of infirmity that may try to work in cahoots with anything on our bloodlines to cause kidney disease, cancer of the kidney, shrinkage of the kidney, and destruction of the kidneys in the name of Jesus Christ. Father, I thank You that the kidneys are functioning accurately now, in the name of Jesus Christ. Dearest Jesus, remove them from dialysis machines in the name of Jesus Christ. Father, cause new kidneys to grow in the place of damaged kidneys, now in the name of Jesus Christ. Shut down every cancer and dialysis center in the name of Jesus Christ. Miracle worker, great I am that I am, come through for Your people in the name of Jesus Christ! Heal bad blood. Filter it out! Clean it out! Heal dialysis ports on bodies. Dry cancers of the kidney up in the name of Jesus Christ! Father, I thank You for a healthy pancreas. We thank you that our pancreas produces the right amount of insulin throughout our bodies in the name of Jesus Christ. I thank You, Lord, that our bodies are not insulin-resistant in the name of Jesus Christ. We command all fatty tissue wrapped around the pancreases, kidneys, hearts, livers, and spleens to dissolve now in the name of Jesus Christ. Father, I thank You that we are whole, healed, and healthy in our bodies, in the name of Jesus Christ. Every organ! Every blood vessel! Every muscle! All tissue! All are healed in the name of Jesus Christ. I thank You, Lord, that it's done, amen!

12

HOLY SPIRIT

Dear Holy Spirit, we revere you! We honor You! You are the very breath of God. We love dwelling with You in the presence of our Heavenly Father. We love commuting with You. We love speaking to You about the truths of our hearts. We know that when we come into Your presence, love will show up. When we come into the presence of God, joy will show up. We know that when we come into Your presence, deliverance will manifest in the room. We desire more of You, Holy Spirit. We desire for Your gentle words to sweep over our hearts like a pure, clean broom. We desire for You to sweep over the gates of our minds and speak to the innermost parts of us. We desire You to show us who the Father is as we enter His presence. We desire for You to show us what the love of the Father is. Holy Spirit, wind of God, blow on us. We desire a fresh wind from the Spirit of the Father. We desire a fresh wind of joy to come upon our hearts in the name of Jesus Christ.

Take us up, Holy Spirit. Take us to the most holy place! Take us to a place of awe and wonder in the presence of our most beautiful Father! We want to go to the most holy place. We want to see His glory. We want to go! Take us up! Take us in! Holy

Spirit, we desire a relationship with You! We desire to know You for who You are, not for what You can give us. We desire fresh revelation, we desire fresh wisdom, and we desire You! Take us up! Take us in! Take us, oh God! Take us in the name of Jesus Christ!

Father, Your Word declares in Acts 2:38, "Peter replied, "Repent and be baptized, every one of you, in the name of Jesus Christ for the forgiveness of your sins. And you will receive the gift of the Holy Spirit." Father, thank You for leaving a part of Yourself here on earth in the form of the Holy Spirit. Thank You for leaving us a comforter. Thank You for leaving Your very Ruah, Your very wind, and Your very voice for us here on earth so that we can have direct access to You in the name of Jesus Christ. Thank You, dear Jesus, for leaving us a keeper. Thank You, oh God. I thank You that Your Spirit has found a home within us. Thank You, Father, for counting us worthy to carry Your Spirit. We are so humbled to have such a privilege to carry Your glory. We are so honored to carry Your wind—the very essence of who You are. Thank You, dearest Jesus. Thank You, Lord. We do not take that lightly.

Thank You for making us clean enough for You to dwell in our bellies. Thank You, Lord, for flowing out of us as rivers of living waters. Thank You for being at home within us. We welcome You and vow to keep our homes (bellies) clean for You to always abide. Father, thank You for pouring out Your Spirit on Your people, God, from the north, south, east, and west. Thank You for pouring Yourself out on Your people again, God, all over this earth, in the name of Jesus Christ. Pour Your Spirit out on the broken, pour it out on the blind, and pour it out on the desolate in the name of Jesus Christ. Rain on us with Your Holy Spirit. God, rain on us with love. Rain on us with Your joy. Lord, we need Your Holy Spirit in the name of Jesus Christ. Rain down Your Spirit in churches again. Rain down Your Spirit in homes again. Draw us with Your Spirit. Draw us with Your love. Draw us, Holy Spirit. Lord, we need You. We need You.

Lord, saturate Your fivefold ascension gifts with Your Spirit. Fill them with the Holy Ghost fire. Bring them into a strong relationship with You. Bring them to a place of intimacy with You, Holy Spirit. Help them to fall in love with the Word of God. Rekindle their desire to pray. Reignite the desire to win souls, Holy Spirit, in the name of Jesus Christ. Pour Yourself, Holy Spirit, over this land like a tsunami. Drench dry places, drench parched lands, drench famine cities and countries. Saturate us. Saturate us! Saturate us! We need a drenching of Your Spirit. Bathe us afresh with Your presence, Holy Spirit. God, let Your Spirit hit schools again. Let Your Spirit hit colleges again in the name of Jesus Christ. God, let Your Spirit hit jailhouses in the name of Jesus Christ. Let Your Spirit walk up and down hospitals and nursing homes! Bring healing and deliverance in the name of Jesus Christ. God, we need You and desire You to pour out Your Spirit upon all of the earth, and Your sons and daughters will prophesy, and by the Spirit of God, we will dream dreams in the name of Jesus Christ. Father, do a holistic work in the land with Your Holy Spirit. We thank You, Lord, that it is so, in Jesus Christ's name we pray, amen!

The Soul of Man

Father, I thank You that Your Word declares in Ezekiel 18:4, "Behold, all souls are mine; as the soul of the father, so also the soul of the son is mine: the soul that sinneth, it shall die." Father, I thank You that since we have confessed our sins and given our full hearts to You, You are faithful and just to forgive us of our sins and cleanse us of all unrighteousness. Father, we thank You that our lives and souls belong to You. We thank You for saving our souls from sin. We thank You for Your precious blood that redeemed us back to You, Jesus. Thank You! I thank You, Lord, for the cleansing of our souls. I thank You, Lord, that Your Spirit consumes us and that nothing about us is alive in the name of Jesus Christ.

Father, I thank You for crucifying our flesh in the name of Jesus Christ. Father, we call souls back to You in the name of Jesus Christ. We stand in the gap for souls that are lost, Father. We thank You for dying for us so that we may have a way back to You. Without Your great sacrifice, there was no way that we could have returned. But because You love us so dearly, You gave Yourself for us. We have a way back home, Father! Thank you.

Father, we pray for broken souls, lost souls, wounded souls, corrupt souls, and prideful souls. We pray that you will heal the broken ones in the name of Jesus Christ. Your Word declares God in Psalms 34:18–22 (KJV), "The LORD is nigh unto them that are of a broken heart; And saveth such as be of a contrite spirit." Father, You are with us. You are with those who are broken. Heal the heart of such, Father. Let them know that You will never leave them or forsake them. Let them know that You saw everything that broke their hearts. Everything that made them cry. Jesus, You saw it. We are to cast our cares upon You, ABBA, for You care for us. Lord, heal the wounded souls. Everything that cut them, great surgeon, stitch them back together with Your love. God, we know that You are able to mend all wounds. Pour in Your oil and love into every place we have been cut deeply, dear Jesus, in the name of Jesus Christ. Lord, thank You for clearing the hearts of the corrupt.

Thank You for taking out all demonic poison that we may have encapsulated during our walk with You in the name of Jesus Christ. We break the covenant with falsehood, wrong teaching, lies, deception, and the pain of the enemy in the name of Jesus Christ. We break covenants with demonic teachings and corrupt seeds of wrongful thinking. Dearest Jesus, purify us. Remove pride and deception from us.

We desire You and only you. Father, we thank You for redeeming the souls of Your people. Bring them home. We call the backsliders back. We call the tired and broken back. We declare and decree that families, cities, and states will come back to You and serve You. Father, we thank You for being the giver of life and our souls belong to You. In the name of Jesus Christ, we pray, amen!

∼

<u>Ending Every Prayer</u>

Father, thank You for meeting us. Your Word declares in Mark 11:24, "Therefore I say unto you, What things soever ye desire, when ye pray, believe that ye receive them, and ye shall have them." Father, I thank You that everything we have prayed and declared is done in the name of Jesus Christ. Father, we bind all of Satan's retaliation and backlash in the name of Jesus Christ. We cancel every contract/hit of the enemy and terminate every assignment in the name of Jesus Christ. We break covenant with every emotional soul tie in the name of Jesus Christ, we pray, amen! And it is so!

13

—————

BONUS PRAYERS

<u>Against Demonic Padlocks and Demonic Lassos:</u>

Prayers against demonic padlocks and demonic lassos Demonic padlocks are dark padlocks sent from Hell to block destiny, purpose, and the blessings of the Lord in your life. They are sent to hinder and delay the plan of God for your life. They often target various parts of the body, such as the ankle, knees, joints, arms, hands, heads, thighs, and even your genital area, in order to block you from walking out the plan of God for your life. Demonic lassos are demonic ropes that are as strong as a thousand natural ropes bound together. They are released by demons of hindrance and bondage in order to bind up the people of God from moving forward in the things of God. Especially a strong preacher of the gospel. Agents of Satan love to sit in the congregation of the saints and release such ropes on the speaker of the hour while they are preaching. It will be hard for the preacher to preach the gospel, work the altar of the Lord Jesus Christ, and even breathe. Let's pray and destroy all demonic padlocks sent from Hell to try to hinder God's people from being delivered and fully used by Him in the name of Jesus Christ.

Father, in the name of Jesus Christ, Your Word declares in John 8:38 that whom the Son sets free is free indeed. It also declares in Isaiah 54:17 that no weapon formed against me shall prosper, and every tongue that rises against us in judgment, You said, we can condemn it in the name of Jesus Christ. Father, I thank You for freedom in You. I thank You that the legal blood of Jesus Christ breaks all strongholds on and over my life and bloodline.

I thank You for being my hammer, my rock, my God, and my fortress. I thank You, Father, that every demonic padlock that Hell has assigned against my life is broken in the name of Jesus Christ. I thank You that every place where I am blocked is loosened NOW in the name of Jesus Christ. Father, I thank You that I will not be hindered in any area of my life. Lord, You created me for a purpose. You created me to win in every area of my life. You created me to be the head and not the tail, only above and not beneath. You have made me the lender, not the borrower. I am Your dear child, and today, I declare freedom in my mind, heart, body, spirit, and soul. I declare and decree that I am a producer, not a procrastinator. I declare and decree that I am a carrier of purpose and a birther of Your promises. I thank You, Lord, that nothing about me will smell the stench of stagnation or delay.

By fire, we roast every demonic padlock around us or attached to us. Lord, I thank You for being the breaker, and I declare and decree that now is my time to come forth. I will not be stopped, hindered, or blocked in the name of Jesus Christ. Freedom, come to my womb now. Freedom, come home now! Freedom, come to my business, children, ministry, and loved ones now in the name of Jesus Christ. Jesus, You are Lord. Nothing or no one else will ever have me bound by demonic cords or ropes. We thank You, Father, that the demonic cords are roasted by fire.

Every demonic padlock or cord that we physically feel attached to or wrapped around any part of our bodies, we release the all-consuming fire of God upon it now in the name of Jesus Christ. Father, I thank You for doing it even now, Lord, in the name of Jesus Christ. We declare and decree that every padlock holding the destinies of our children and their freedom is broken now in the name of Jesus Christ. Lord, I thank You that every demonic padlock released upon us to hinder our worship and block our frequency unto You is destroyed now, in the name of Jesus Christ. Father, I thank You for joy! Father, I thank You! We thank You, Lord! We thank You, dearest Jesus! Father, we thank You that every demonic padlock that has stopped Your people from moving forward in any area of their lives is broken now in the name of Jesus Christ. Father, we thank You that it is done. We give You thanks for the ability to lift our hands and give You praise. No more ropes. No more chains. No more shackles. No more! We are free, and we live like it, walk like it, walk in it, and stand on it, Father, in the name of Jesus Christ, amen.

9 789655 786118